# Software Patterns Made Easy

Justice Nanhou

# Table of Contents

# Disclaimer

**Software Patterns Made Easy**



While the author has taken the utmost efforts to ensure the accuracy of the written content, all readers are advised to follow the information stated therein at their own risk. The author will not be held responsible for any individual or economic damage caused by the misunderstanding of information. All readers of this book are encouraged to seek expert advice when required.

This book has been written for informational purposes only. Efforts have been made to make this book as comprehensive and precise as possible. Nevertheless, there may be mistakes in typography or content. Also, this book provides information only up to the publishing date. Therefore, this book should be used as a guide - not as the ultimate source.

The primary purpose of this book is to teach readers about the topic being discussed. The writer and the publisher do not warrant that the information contained in this book is

# Acknowledgments

To all the individuals I have had the opportunity to lead, be led by, or watch their leadership from afar, I want to thank you for inspiring and motivating me.

I would like to thank my lovely parents, Louisette and Jean Nanhou. My tutor and second father, Christian Seudieu and his family for their advice.

Having an idea and turning it into a book is as hard as it sounds. The experience is both internally challenging and rewarding. I want to thank the individuals that helped make this happen, especially Walter Krasniqi, Ryan Fernandez and their amazing publishing team.

Finally, the heavenly father for inspiration and daily strength.

# Introduction

If you are ever writing code and get the funny feeling that you have solved the problem you were working on before, you probably have! You might well have come across the same kind of situation in the past, felt puzzled about it, and came up with a solution to that problem. This might have happened quite a few times.

However, why keep reinventing the wheel?

Why don't you just write down your solutions and refer back to it as needed? That is what design patterns are all about. A design pattern represents a solution to the problem or a class of problems that one can put to work at once in your code. As a matter of fact, design patterns go one step further: they also help you share the solutions discovered by other programmers.

The design patterns you will see in this book represent the insightful solutions to the dilemmas that just about every programmer faces every now and then. Knowing these design patterns is going to save you a lot of time as well as efforts. All you need to understand is that someone has already solved the problem for you with a careful eye towards good programming practices and efficiency. All you have to do is apply that solution to your own code.

The design patterns I have covered in this book are essential for any programmer to understand. There is a lot of ad hoc programming which goes on in this world, which can lead to a lot of errors in critical code. Why should you be the one sitting in front of the debugger every single day? We have put design patterns to work for you, which you can just slip as a solution into place.

# WHAT ARE DESIGN PATTERNS AND WHY DO YOU NEED THEM

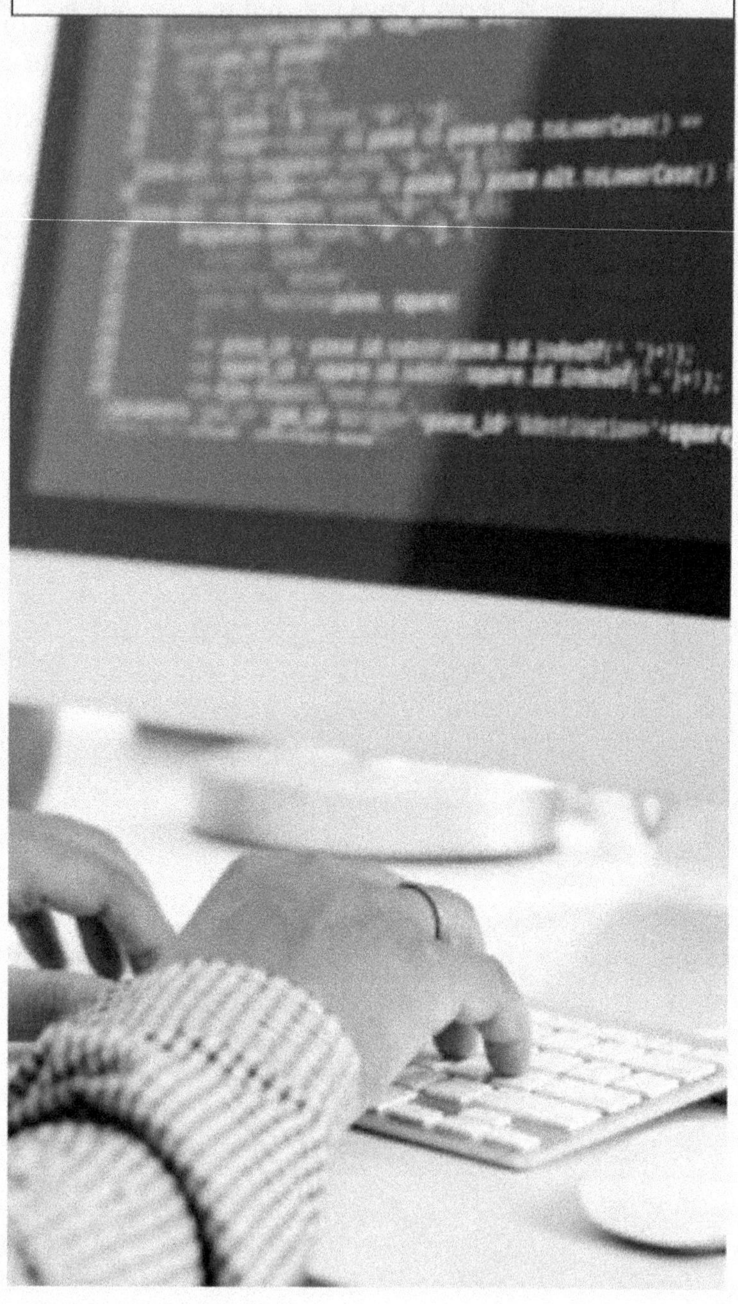

# What Are Design Patterns and Why Do You Need Them?

As a programmer, you know how easy it can be to get lost in the details of what you are doing. However, if you lose the overview, do not plan effectively, and lose sight of the bigger picture, the code you are writing ends up working just fine for a while, however, unless you understand the bigger picture, that code is a specialised solution to any particular problem.

Developers typically regard their work as tackling individual problems by writing code to solve them. However, the truth is that in any expert environment, developers almost always end up spending a lot of time on maintenance and adapting code to suit new situations while writing an entirely new code.

Even though software professionals might be familiar with the term 'design patterns' there are many who have simply no idea regarding where they come from and what they indeed are. Subsequently, some people fail to see the value and benefits these design patterns bring to the overall software development process, especially in areas pertaining to maintenance and code reuse.

Design patterns can be defined as time tested solutions to recurring issues.

Through this chapter, I will try to bridge this gap by defining design patterns and summarizing their salient features to arrive at a working definition. This will help you understand what design patterns essentially are and what one should expect while incorporating them into the designs. Finally, this chapter will explicitly summarise the benefits design patterns bring to software development and why you should use them in your work.

## What Are Design Patterns and Where Do They Originate From

Design patterns can be defined as time tested solutions to recurring issues. The term refers to both the description of a solution you can read, along with an instance of the solution which can be used to solve a particular problem. Design patterns stem from the work of Christopher Alexander, who was a civil engineer who wrote about his experience when it comes to solving design-related issues.

It occurred to Alexander that some design constructs, when used time and again, can lead to the desired effect. He documented and published his wisdom and experience so that others could benefit from it. Approximately 15 years ago, software professionals began to incorporate Alexander's principles into the creation of early design pattern documentation as a guide to the novice developers.

Design patterns can be represented as the relationship between classes and objects with defined responsibilities that act in consort to carry out the solution. In order to illustrate a design pattern, you can consider the Adapter pattern, which is one of the original 23 patterns described in the Design Patterns published by Erich Gamma, Richard Helm, Ralph Johnson, and John Vlissides in their seminal 1995 book, Design Pattern: Elements of Reusable Object-Oriented Software.

The design pattern community has grown both in membership as well as coverage.

The adapter offers an effective solution to the scenario in which a client and server are required to interact with one another; however, it cannot because their interfaces are incompatible. To implement an Adapter, you must create a custom class that honours the interface provided by the server and defines the server operations as per the client expectations. This is a much better solution than altering the client to match the server interface.

The design pattern community has grown both in membership as well as coverage. The pattern literature describes new patterns to solve emerging issues that are related to technological advancements. As a software professional, you are the beneficiary of this body of knowledge. In order to use these patterns, you are going to need to learn them and become familiar with them so that you understand which pattern you can pull from your toolbox when any design related issues arise.

Numerous patterns have been documented over the years. These patterns have been classified in different ways. Take your time in order to learn different ways to classify design patterns as you will gain greater insight into them. As you enhance your pattern knowledge, it would be a good idea to develop your own classification system to reflect how you utilise them.

## Structure of a Design Pattern

Design pattern documentation is exceptionally structured. These patterns are documented from a template that identifies all the information required to understand the software issues along with the solutions in terms of the relationships between the classes and objects necessary to implement the solution. There is no uniform agreement within the design pattern community on how you can describe a pattern template.

| Term | Description |
| --- | --- |
| Pattern Name | Describes the essence of the pattern in a short, but expressive, name |
| Intent | Describes what the pattern does |
| Also Known As | List any synonyms for the pattern |
| Motivation | Provides an example of a problem and how the pattern solves that problem |
| Applicability | Lists the situations where the pattern is applicable |
| Structure | Set of diagrams of the classes and objects that depict the pattern |
| Participants | Describes the classes and objects that participate in the design pattern and their responsibilities |
| Collaborations | Describes how the participants collaborate to carry out their responsibilities |
| Consequences | Describes the forces that exist with the pattern and the benefits, trade-offs, and the variable that is isolated by the pattern |

The template mentioned above captures all the essential information that is required to recognise the essence of the problem as well as the structure of the solution. Numerous pattern templates have less structure than this but fundamentally cover the same content.

## Benefits of Design Patterns

The design pattern has two significant advantages. Firstly, they offer individuals an effective way through which they can resolve issues related to software development through a proven solution. This solution facilitates the development of highly cohesive modules with minimal coupling. They isolate the variability that might exist in the system requirements, which makes the overall system a lot easier to understand and maintain.

Secondly, design patterns make communications between designers more efficient. Software professionals can immediately picture the higher-level design when they refer to the name of the pattern used to solve any particular problem when it comes to discussing the system design.

# CREATIONAL DESIGN PATTERNS

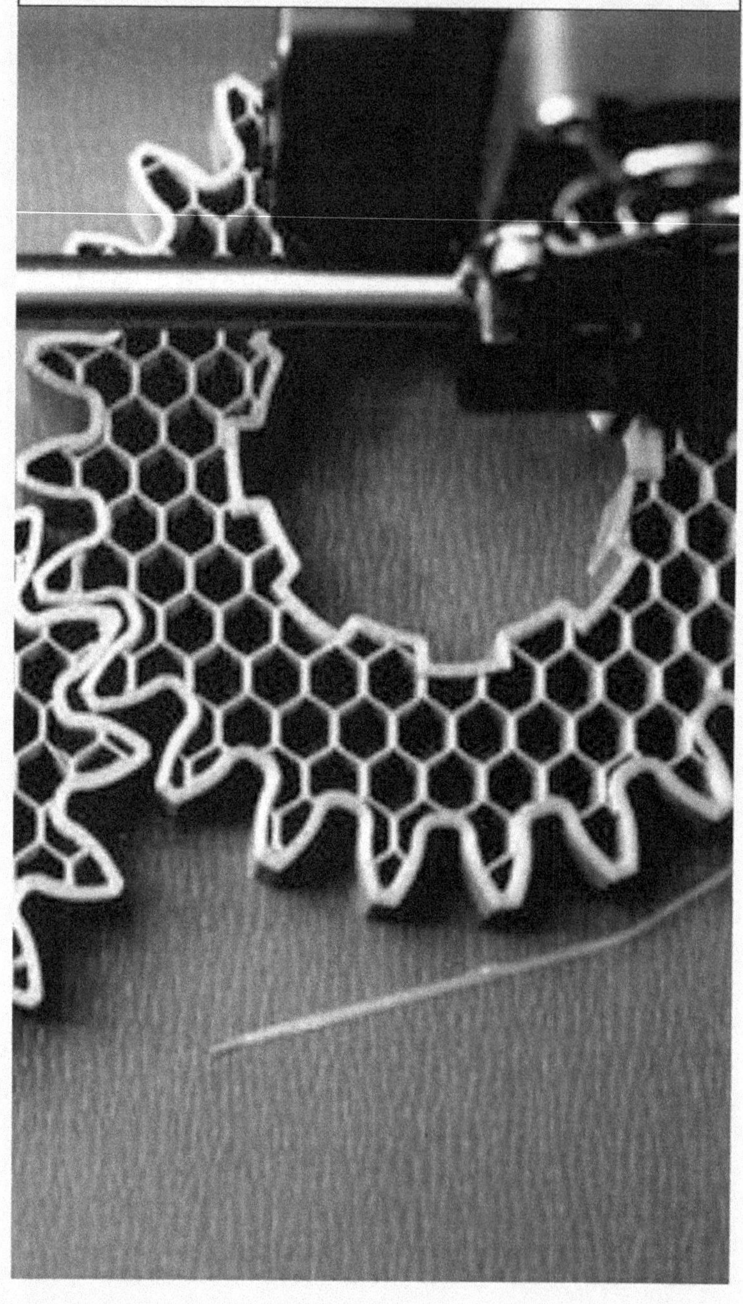

# Creational Design Patterns

Many of these design trends are for instantiation of class. This trend can be further split into patterns of entity formation and patterns of item development. While inheritance is effectively used by class-creation patterns in the instantiation process, object-creation patterns effectively use delegation to get the work done.

## Abstract Factory

It is to provide an interface to construct linked or dependent entity families without defining their specific groups. A structure that encapsulates: several potential "platforms," and a set of "things" being developed. A Factory now characterises a "family" of objects that it can create. This family of objects created by factory is determined at run-time according to the selection of concrete factory class. In this case client doesn't know which concrete object it gets from each of factories, since it used only the generic interfaces of their products. This pattern is very good when you need to separate the details of objects instantiation. In general factories may have more than one factory method. Each factory method encapsulates the new operator and the concrete, platform-specific, product classes. Each platform is then modeled with a factory derived class.

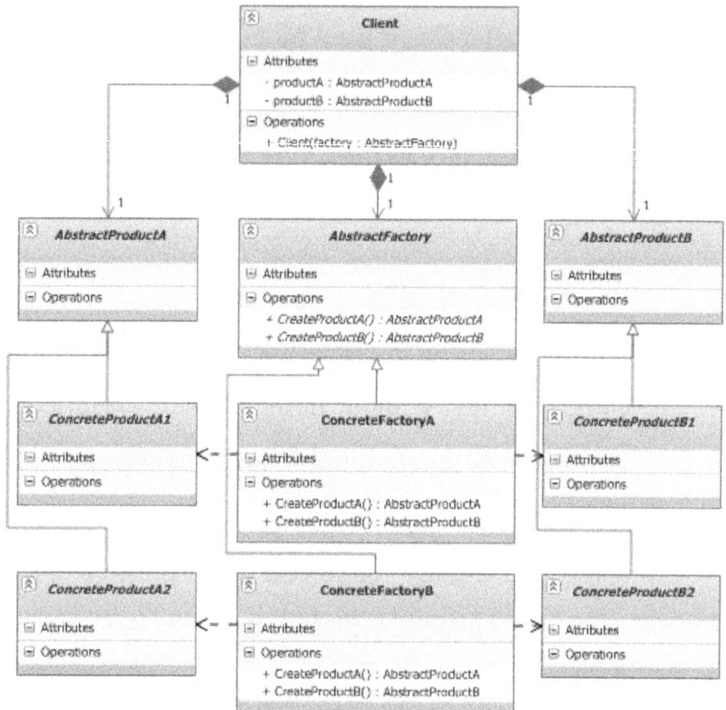


**Figure 2.1**

***Abstract Family Structural Code***

The diagram above describes an implementation of the abstract factory design pattern. This diagram consists of five classes:

**Client**

This class uses interfaces declared by AbstractFactory and AbstractProduct classes.

**AbstractFactory**

This is an abstract base for all concrete factory classes that will generate new related objects. For each type of objects that will be instantiated a method is included within this.

**ConcreteFactory**

This class is inherited from AbstractFactory class. ConcreteFactory overrides methods of AbstractFactory that will generate a new related object. In case when AbstractFactroy is an interface, this class must implement all members of factory interface.

**AbstractProduct**

This class is base class for all types of objects that factory can create.

### ConcreteProduct

This is a concrete implementation of AbstractProduct class. There can by a multiple class which derives from AbstractProduct class with specific functionality[1].

## Builder

Builder design pattern is a pattern that separates the creation of a complex entity from its image, such that separate representations may be generated from the same design method. This parses a dynamic representation, produces one of many targets. Builder pattern builds a complex object using simple objects and using a step by step approach. This type of design pattern comes under creational pattern as this pattern provides one of the best ways to create an object. A Builder class builds the final object step by step. This builder is independent of other objects.

[1]Robert, K. (2012). Design Patterns 1 of 3 - Creational Design Patterns. Code Project. Retrieved from: https://www.codeproject.com/Articles/430590/Design-Patterns-1-of-3-Creational-Design-Patterns

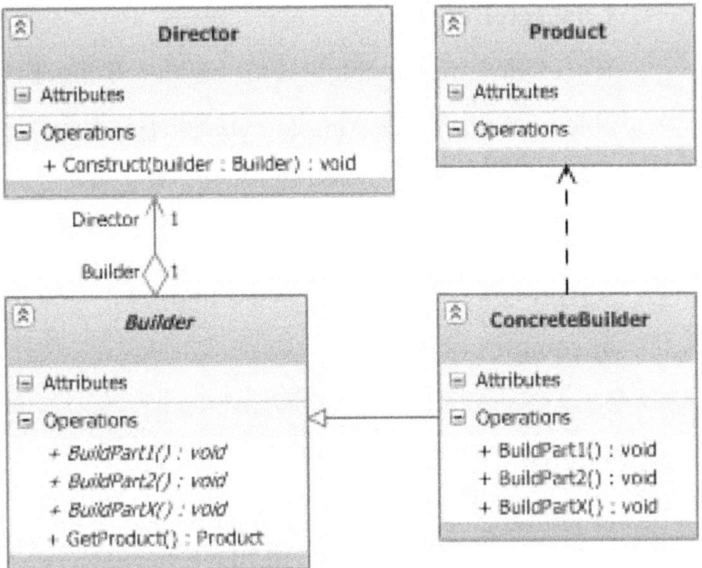


**Figure 2.2**

***Builder Structural Code***

The diagram above explains the implementation of the builder design pattern. This diagram consists of four classes:

**Product**

It represents the complex object that is being built.

**Builder**

This is base class (or interface) for all builders and defines a step that must be taken in order to correctly create a complex object (product). Generally, each step is an abstract method that is overridden by concrete implementation.

### ConcreteBuilder

It provides implementation for builder. Builder is an object able to create other complex objects (products).

### Director

It represents class that controls algorithm used for creation of complex object[2].

## Factory Method

It defines an entity development method, however let subclasses determine which instance to instantiate. Factory Process lets subclasses undergo a class postpone instantiation. Factory pattern is one of the most used design patterns in Java. This type of design pattern comes under creational pattern as this pattern provides one of the best ways to create an object. In Factory pattern, we create object without exposing the creation logic to the client and refer to newly created object using a common interface. This pattern is also known as Virtual Constructor pattern. The factory method pattern defines an interface for creating an object and leaves the choice of type to the subclasses. Factory method design pattern makes a design more customizable and only a little complicated. Other design patterns require

---

[2]Robert, K. (2012). Design Patterns 1 of 3 - Creational Design Patterns. Code Project. Retrieved from: https://www.codeproject.com/Articles/430590/Design-Patterns-1-of-3-Creational-Design-Patterns

new classes, whereas factory method only requires a new operation.

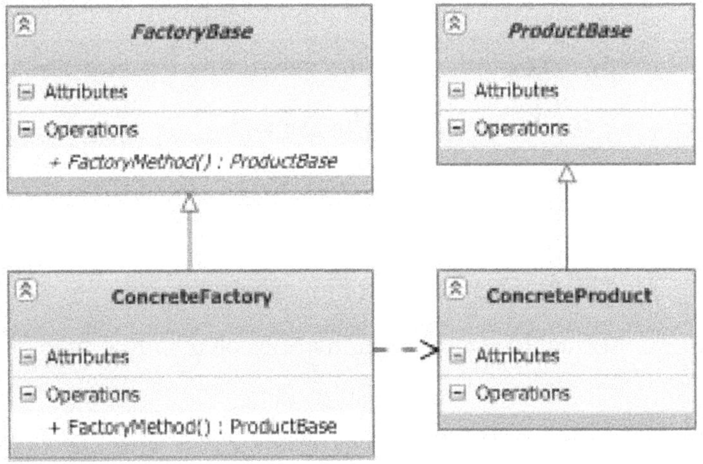


**Figure 2.3**

***Factory Method Structural Code***

The diagram above describes an implementation of the factory method design pattern. This diagram consists of four classes:

**FactoryBase**

This is an abstract class for the concrete factory classes which will return new objects. In some cases, it could be a simple interface containing the signature for the factory method. This class contains FactoryMethod which returns a ProductBase object.

**ConcreteFactory**

It represents concrete implementation of factory. Usually, this class overrides the generating FactoryMethod and returns a ConcreteProduct object.

**ProductBase**

This is a base class for all products created by concrete factories. In some cases, it could be a simple interface.

**ConcreteProduct**

This is a concrete implementation of ProducBase. Concrete product classes can include specific functionality. These objects are created by factory methods[3].

## Prototype

The prototype design pattern is a pattern that is used to instantiate a class by copying, or cloning, the properties of an existing object. The new object is an exact copy of the prototype but permits modification without altering the original.

---

[3]Robert, K. (2012). Design Patterns 1 of 3 - Creational Design Patterns. Code Project. Retrieved from: https://www.codeproject.com/Articles/430590/Design-Patterns-1-of-3-Creational-Design-Patterns

Prototype patterns is required, when object creation is time consuming, and costly operation, so an object is created with the help of an existing object. One of the best available ways to create object from existing objects are clone() method. Clone is the simplest approach to implement prototype pattern. However, it is up to the programmer to decide how to copy existing object based on the business model.

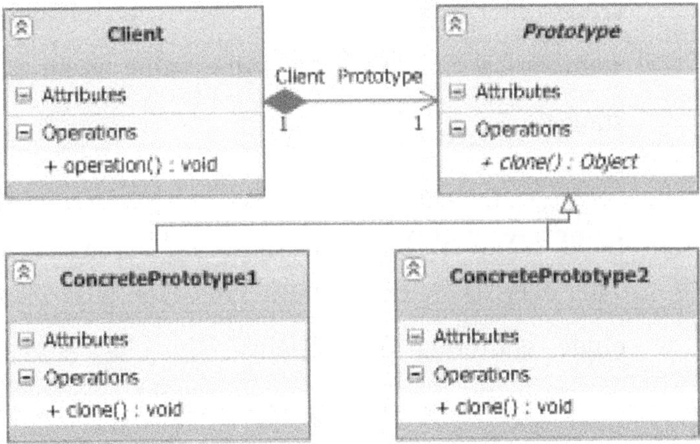


**Figure 2.4**

***Prototype Structural Code***

The diagram above describes an implementation of the prototype design pattern. This diagram consists of two type of classes:

**Prototype**

It represents an abstract base class from the objects that can be cloned. This class contains single virtual method Clone() that returns prototype object. .NET framework includes interface named ICloneable which creates a new instance of a class with the same value as an existing instance.

**ConcretePrototype**

This class is inherited from Prototype base class and includes additional functionality. This class is also overridden Clone() method[4].

## Singleton

The singleton design pattern is a pattern that is used to ensure that a class can only have one concurrent instance. Whenever additional objects of a singleton class are required, the previously created, single instance is provided. Sometimes we need to have only one instance of our class

---

[4]Robert, K. (2012). Design Patterns 1 of 3 - Creational Design Patterns. Code Project. Retrieved from: https://www.codeproject.com/Articles/430590/Design-Patterns-1-of-3-Creational-Design-Patterns

for example a single DB connection shared by multiple objects as creating a separate DB connection for every object may be costly. In ASP.NET, HttpContext class is a nice example of singleton. Base idea of singleton pattern is to centralise management of internal or external resources and to provide a global point of access to the resources.

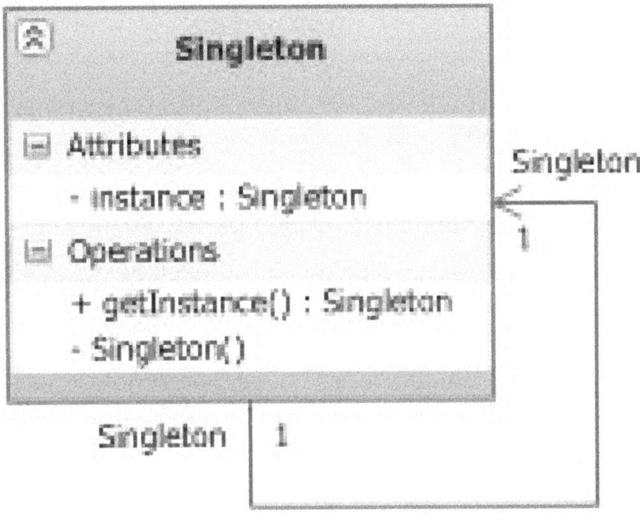


**Figure 2.5**

***Singleton Structural Code***

Figure 2.5 above describes an implementation of the singleton design pattern. This diagram consists of only one class:

**Singleton:**

This class is a static method called GetSingleton which returns the single instance held in private variable[5].

[5]Robert, K. (2012). Design Patterns 1 of 3 - Creational Design Patterns. Code Project. Retrieved from: https://www.codeproject.com/Articles/430590/Design-Patterns-1-of-3-Creational-Design-Patterns

# STRUCTURAL DESIGN PATTERNS

# Structural Design Patterns

All of these architecture trends are about composition of class and entity. Inheritance is used to design interfaces via structured class-creation patterns. Structural object-patterns describe how artifacts may be constructed to obtain new features.

## Adapter

Adapter is a design pattern that converts a user interface into another intended application interface. Connection lets groups function together regardless of conflicting implementations, which couldn't otherwise. Adapter is about building an intermediary abstraction that converts the old portion into the new structure, or maps it to. On the Adapter object, clients call methods which redirect them to calls to the legacy portion. The technique will either be applied with succession or grouping. The Adapter design enables mutually incompatible groups to operate together by transforming the one-class framework into a framework the clients anticipate. Socket wrenches offer the Adapter as an example. A connector is connected to a ratchet, so the drive size is equal. Across the USA common drive ratios are 1/2 "to 1/4." A 1/2 "drive ratchet would naturally not fit into a

1/4" drive socket when you use an adapter. A 1/2 "to 1/4" connector is fitted with a 1/2 "female attachment for the 1/2" drive ratchet and a 1/4 "male link for the 1/4" drive port.

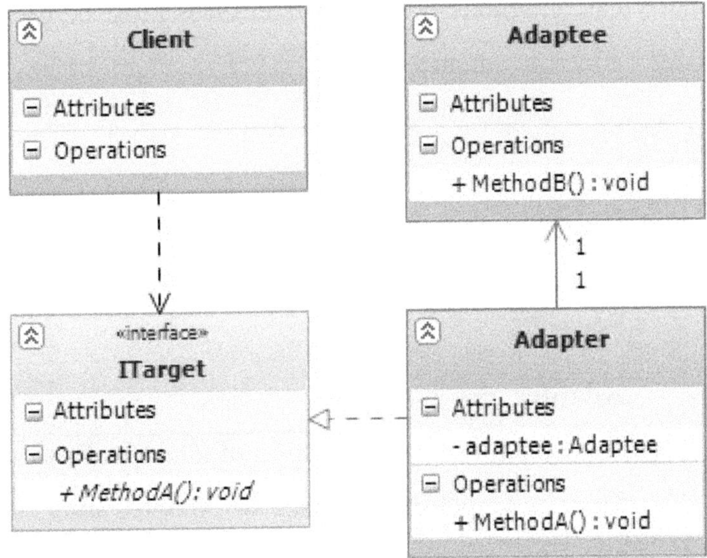


**Figure 3.1**

***Adapter Structural Code***

The diagram above explains an implementation of the adapter design pattern. Diagram consists of four parts:

**Client**

It represents the class which need to use an incompatible interface. This incompatible interface is implemented by Adaptee.

**ITarget**

It defines a domain-specific interface that client uses. In this case it is a simple interface, but in some situations it could be an abstract class which adapter inherits. In this case methods of this abstract class must be overriden by concrete adapter.

**Adaptee**

It represents a class provides a functionality that is required by client.

**Adapter**

It is concrete implementation of adapter. This class translates incompatible interface of Adaptee into interface of Client[6].

## Bridge

Bridge pattern is a design pattern that decouples a concept from applying it to enable the two to differ independently. Bridge pattern is very valuable pattern because it allows you to separate abstract elements of class from the implementation details. Sometimes an implementation can have

---

[6]Robert, K. (2012). Design Patterns 2 of 3 – Structural Design Patterns. Code Project. Retrieved from: https://www.codeproject.com/Articles/438922/Design-Patterns-2-of-3-Structural-Design-Patterns

two or more different implementations. Let's consider a program that handles persistence of objects on different platforms. Some of objects should be saved into database and other objects into file system. When simply extends the program with this functionality, it could cause problems because we binds abstraction with implementation. In this case, it is more suitable to use Bridge pattern and separate abstraction from its implementation.

One of the biggest benefits of Bridge pattern is its ability to change implementation details at run time. This could permit the user to switch implementations to determine how the software interoperates with other systems.

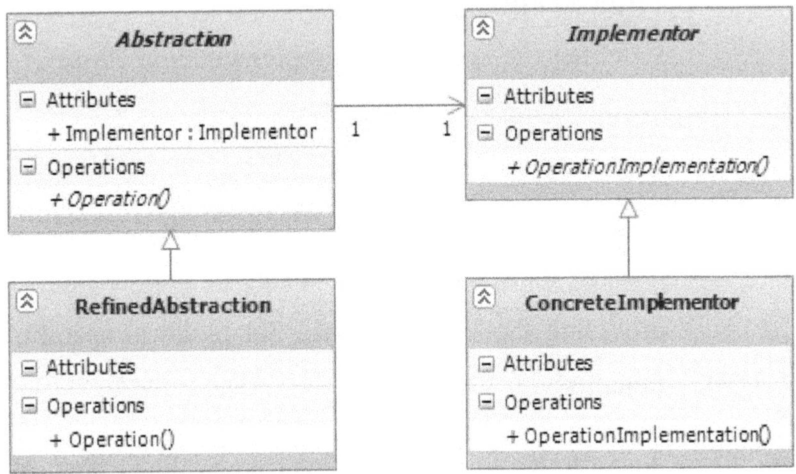


**Figure 3.8**

***Bridge Structrural Code***

The diagram above explains an implementation of the bridge design pattern. Diagram consists of four parts:

**Abstraction**

It defines an abstraction interface. It acts as base class for other refined abstraction classes. It also holds reference to particular implementation that it is using for platform specific functionality.

**RefinedAbstraction**

It provides more specific variations upon abstraction but it doesn't contain any implementation details. De facto it only extends abstraction.

**Implementor**

It defines the interface for implementation classes.

**ConcreteImplementor**

This class inherits from RefinedAbstraction class. There may be more than one instances of Implementor classes providing the same interface but platform specific functionality[7].

---

[7]Robert, K. (2012). Design Patterns 2 of 3 – Structural Design Patterns. Code Project. Retrieved from: https://www.codeproject.com/Articles/438922/Design-Patterns-2-of-3-Structural-Design-Patterns

## Composite

It composes artifacts that reflect whole-part hierarchies into tree structures. Composite lets specific artifacts and entity configurations be viewed equally by clients. The key concept is that you can manipulate a single instance of the object just as you would manipulate a group of them. The operations you can perform on all the composite objects often have a least common denominator relationship.

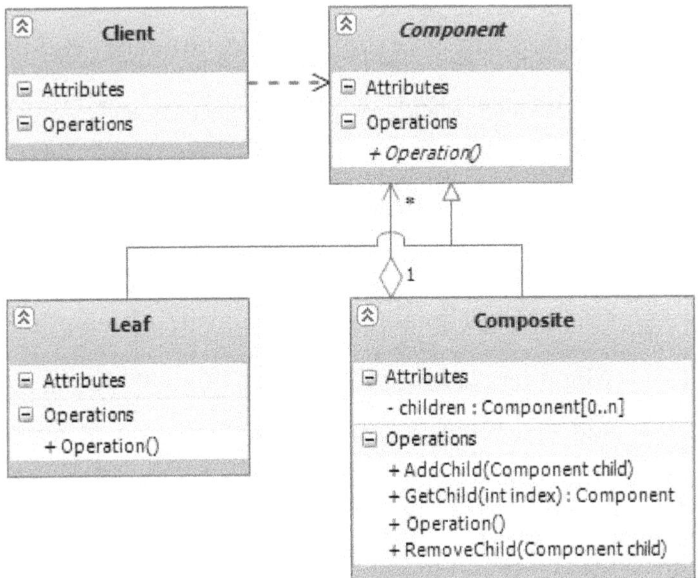


**Figure 3.3**

***Composite Structural Code***

Composite pattern has four participants:

**Client**

It manipulates the objects in the composition through the component interface.

**Component**

It is an abstraction for all components, including composite ones. It declares the interface for objects in the composition. Sometimes it defines an interface for accessing a component's parent in the recursive structure, and implements it if that's appropriate.

**Composite**

This is a key element of this design pattern. It represent a Composite components. Composite element are elements which have child elements. It implements the methods to add and remove children elements and it implements all Component methods, generally by delegating them to its children.

### Leaf

It represents leaf objects in the composition and implements all Component methods[8].

## Decorator

Decorator pattern allows a user to add new functionality to an existing object without altering its structure. This type of design pattern comes under structural pattern as this pattern acts as a wrapper to existing class. This pattern creates a decorator class which wraps the original class and provides additional functionality keeping class methods signature intact.

---

[8]Robert, K. (2012). Design Patterns 2 of 3 – Structural Design Patterns. Code Project. Retrieved from: https://www.codeproject.com/Articles/438922/Design-Patterns-2-of-3-Structural-Design-Patterns

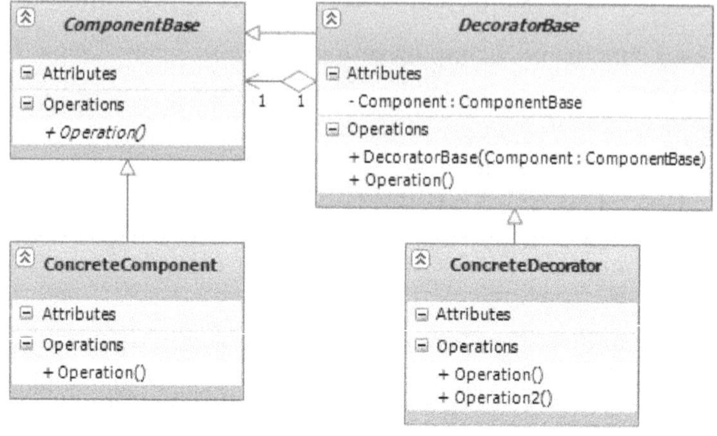


**Figure 3.4**

***Decorator Structural Code***

## Façade

The facade pattern is a design pattern that is used to simplify access to functionality in complex or poorly designed subsystems. The facade class provides a simple, single-class interface that hides the implementation details of the underlying code. Facade pattern is generally used to simplify interface to a larger body of code. This pattern is very helpful when you deal with many independent classes or classes that require the use of multiple methods, especially when they are difficult to use or difficult to understand. We can tell that facade pattern is some kind of wrapper that contains a set of members they are easy to understand and use. This pattern is used when wrapped subsystem is poorly designed and you can have no possibility to refactor its code. Facade pattern makes software library easier to use, understand and test. It makes library more readable and can reduce dependencies.

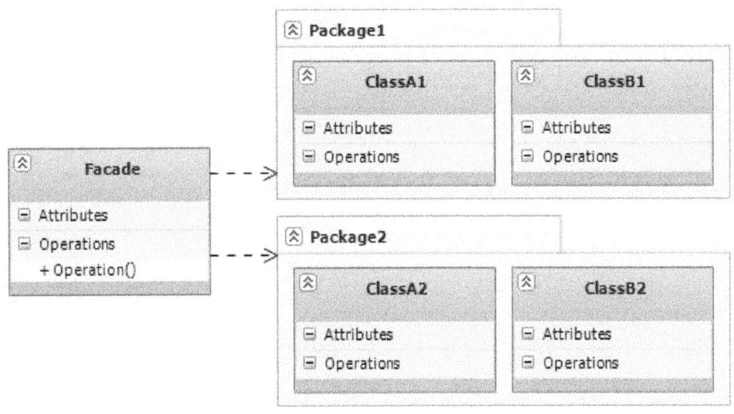


**Figure 3.5**

***Façade Structural Code***

Façade design pattern consists of following three parts:

**Facade**

This class contains the set of simple functions that are made available to its users and that hide the complexities of the difficult-to-use subsystems.

**PackageA/B**

The complex functionality that is accessed via the facade class does not necessary reside in a single assembly. The packages in the diagram illustrate this, as each can be an assembly containing classes.

**ClassA/B**

These classes contain the functionality that is being presented via the facade[9].

---

[9]Robert, K. (2012). Design Patterns 2 of 3 – Structural Design Patterns. Code Project. Retrieved from: https://www.codeproject.com/Articles/438922/Design-Patterns-2-of-3-Structural-Design-Patterns

# BEHAVIORAL DESIGN PATTERNS

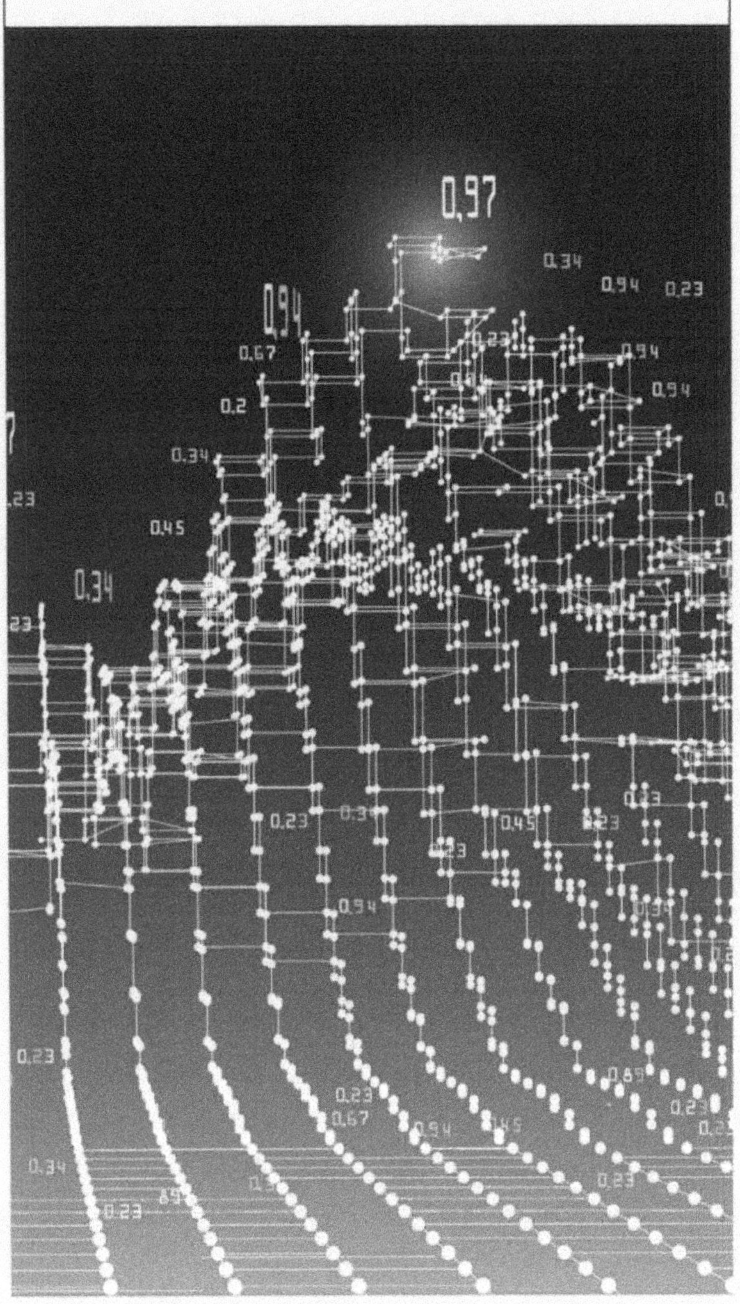

# Behavioural Design Patterns

Such architecture trends also contribute to the contact of artifacts through Gender. Behavioural trends are certain behaviours that deal with contact between individuals in the most common manner.

## Chain of Responsibility

It is to stop pairing the source of an application with its recipient by allowing more than one entity the ability to manage the submission. Group the items that are getting and move the question down the chain before an entity manages them. Structure: The derived classes are able to satisfy requests from the Client. If the "new" item is not accessible or necessary, it delegates to the base unit, which delegates to the "next" entity, and the life-circle begins. Multiple handlers could help handle any order. The order should be transferred across the whole chain, the last link being diligent not to transfer to an "empty next."

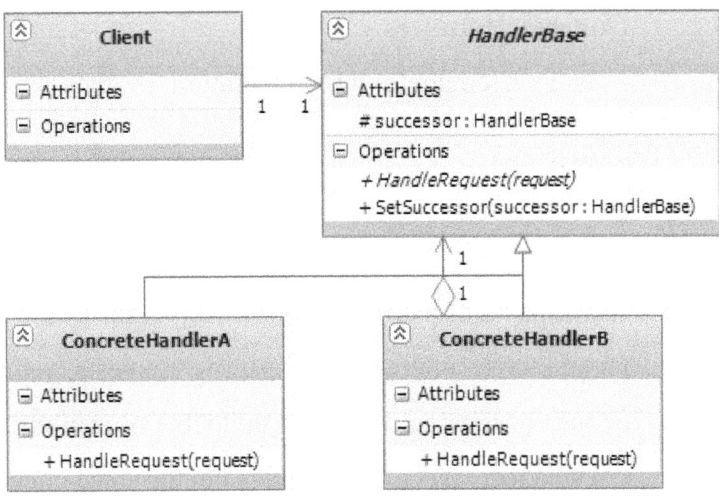


**Figure 4.1**

***Chain of Responsibility Structural Code***

Chain of responsibility pattern has three participants:

**Client**

This class passes commands (or requests) to the first object of the chain of processing objects.

**HandlerBase**

It represents an interface or base class for all concrete handlers. It contains a member variable which points to the next processing object.

### ConcreteHandlers

This is a concrete implementation of the HandlerBase class[10].

## Command

It encapsulates a program as an entity, thus enabling you to parameterise clients with specific requests, requests for queues or logs, and endorse undoable operations. The client which creates a command is not the same client executing it. This distinction allows for versatility in order timing and sequencing. Materializing commands as objects ensures they can, like every other entity, be transferred, set, exchanged, loaded onto a table and otherwise instrumented or controlled.

Command artifacts should be viewed as "tokens" generated by one client who understands what needs to be achieved and moved on to another client who has the ability to do so.

---

[10]Robert, K. (2012). Design Patterns 3 of 3 – Structural Design Patterns. Code Project. Retrieved from: https://www.codeproject.com/Articles/455228/Design-Patterns-3-of-3-Behavioural-Design-Patterns

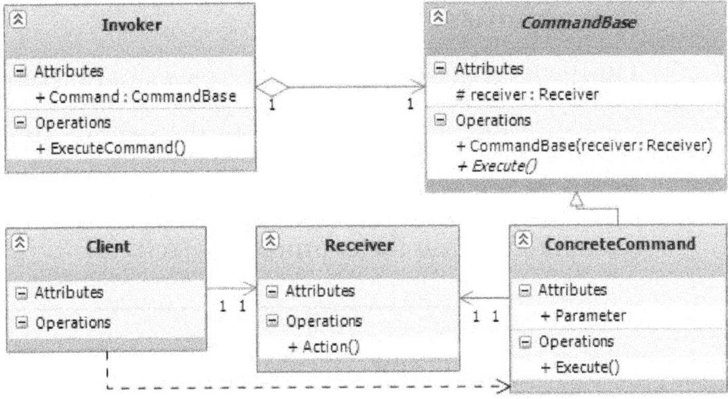


**Figure 4.2**

***Command Structural Code***

Image 4.2 describes an implementation of the command design pattern. This diagram consists of five parts:

**Client**

The class is a consumer of the classes of the Command design pattern. It creates the command objects and links them to receivers.

**Receiver**

This is the class which knows how to perform the operations associated with carrying out the request.

### CommandBase

This is the abstract class (or interface) for all command objects. It holds information about the receiver which is responsible for executing an operation using information encapsulated within the command object.

### ConcreteCommand

It is concrete implementation of the CommandBase abstract class or interface.

### Invoker

It is the object which decides when to execute the command[11].

## Interpreter

It defines a representation for its grammar, given a language, along with an interpreter who uses the representation to interpret sentences in the language. It attaches a scope to a vocabulary, the vocabulary to a grammar and the grammar to an object-oriented hierarchical architecture. Interpreter suggests a recursive grammatical modeling of the domain. Each rule in grammar is either a 'composite' (a rule

---

[11]Robert, K. (2012). Design Patterns 3 of 3 – Structural Design Patterns. Code Project. Retrieved from: https://www.codeproject.com/Articles/455228/Design-Patterns-3-of-3-Behavioural-Design-Patterns

that refers to other rules) or a terminal (a tree-structured leaf node). Interpreter relies on the Composite pattern's recursive traversal to interpret the 'sentences' that it is asked to process.

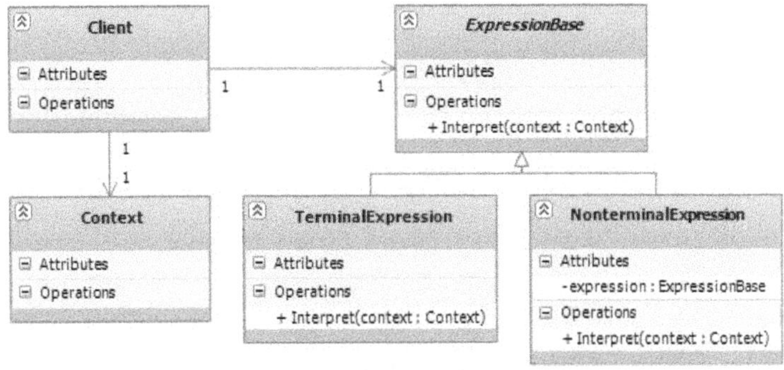


**Figure 4.3**

***Interpreter Structural Code***

Interpreter has five classes:

**Client**

It builds (or is given) an abstract syntax tree representing a particular sentence in the language that the grammar defines. The abstract syntax tree is assembled from instances of the NonterminalExpression and TerminalExpression classes invoking the Interpret operation.

**Context**

It contains information that is global to the interpreter.

**ExpressionBase**

It declares an interface or abstract class for all expressions.

**TerminalExpresion**

It implements an Interpret operation associated with terminal symbols in the grammar. An instance is required for every terminal symbol in the sentence.

**NonterminalExpressions**

Non-terminal expressions are represented using a concrete subclass of ExpressionBase. These expressions are aggregates containing one or more further expressions, each of which may be terminal or non-terminal. When a non-terminal expression class interpret method is called, the process of interpretation includes calls to the Interpret method of the expressions it holds[12].

---

[12]Robert, K. (2012). Design Patterns 3 of 3 – Structural Design Patterns. Code Project. Retrieved from: https://www.codeproject.com/Articles/455228/Design-Patterns-3-of-3-Behavioural-Design-Patterns

## Strategy

The strategy pattern is a design pattern that permits a set of similar algorithms to be defined and encapsulated in their own classes. The algorithm to be used for a particular purpose may then be selected at run-time according to your requirements. This design pattern can be used in common situations where classes differ only in behaviour. In this case it is a good idea to separate these behaviour algorithms in separate classes which can be selected at run-time. This pattern defines a family of algorithms, encapsulates each one, and makes them interchangeable. This separation allows behaviours may vary independently of clients that use it. It also increases the flexibility of the application allowing to add new algorithms in future.

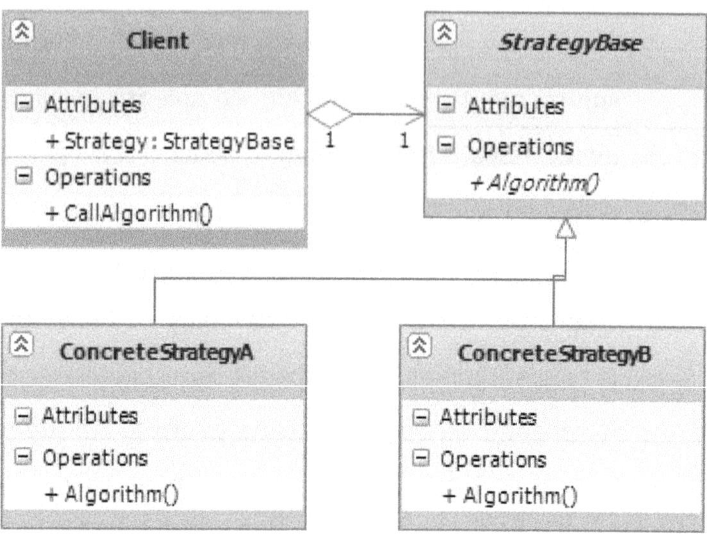


**Figure 4.4**

***Strategy Structural Code***

Strategy consists of three parts:

**Client**

This class uses interchangeable algorithms. It maintains a reference to the StrategyBase object. Sometimes it defines an interface that lets StrategyBase access its data.

**StrategyBase**

It declares an interface common to all supported algorithms. The client uses this interface to call the algorithm defined by a ConcreteStrategy.

**ConcreteStrategy**

This is the concrete strategy class inherited from the StrategyBase class. Each instance provides a different algorithm that may be used by the client[13].

## Visitor Pattern

The visitor pattern is a design pattern that separates a set of structured data from the functionality that may be performed upon it. This promotes loose coupling and enables additional operations to be added without modifying the data classes.

The Visitor pattern allows you to separate an algorithm from a relatively complex object structure on which it operates. The result of this separation is a data model with limited functionality and a set of visitors that perform operations upon the data. Another benefit is the ability to add a new visitor without modifying the existing structure. The classes of data structures are created with members that can be consumed by the visitor object. Usually this data object is passed to the visitor as a parameter of its method (the convention is to call this method Visit()).

[13]Robert, K. (2012). Design Patterns 3 of 3 – Structural Design Patterns. Code Project. Retrieved from: https://www.codeproject.com/Articles/455228/Design-Patterns-3-of-3-Behavioural-Design-Patterns

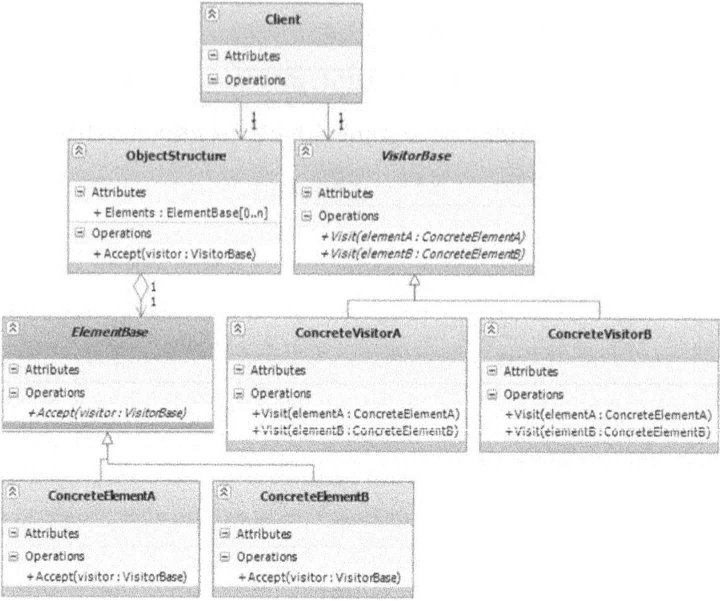


**Figure 4.5**

***Visitor Structural Code***

Visitor design pattern has the following six elements:

Client: this class is a consumer of the Visitor pattern. It manages the object structure and instructs the objects within the structure when to accept a visitor.

**ObjectStructure:**

This is a class containing all the objects that can be visited. It offers a mechanism to iterate through all the elements. This structure is not necessarily a collection. In can be a complex structure, such as a composite object.

**ElementBase**

It is an abstraction which declares the accept operation. This is the entry point which enables an object to be "visited" by the visitor object. Each object from a collection should implement this abstraction in order to be able to be visited.

**ConcreteElement**

These classes inherit from the base abstract class ElementBase or implement an interface and defines the accept operation. The visitor object is passed to this object using the accept operation.

**VisitorBase:**

It declares a Visit operation for each class of ConcreteElement in the object structure. The operation's name and signature identifies the class that sends the Visit request to the visitor. That lets the visitor determine the concrete class of the element being visited. Then the visitor can access the elements directly through its particular interface.

**ConcreteVisitor**

It implements each operation declared by a Visitor. Each operation implements a fragment of the algorithm defined for the corresponding class or object in the structure. ConcreteVisitor provides the context for the algorithm and stores its local state. This state often accumulates results during the traversal of the structure[14].

[14]Robert, K. (2012). Design Patterns 3 of 3 – Structural Design Patterns. Code Project. Retrieved from: https://www.codeproject.com/Articles/455228/Design-Patterns-3-of-3-Behavioural-Design-Patterns

# HOW CAN YOU APPLY DESIGN PATTERNS

# How Can You Apply Design Patterns

In software engineering, a design pattern can be described as a general repeatable solution to a commonly occurring problem in software design. A design pattern is not a finished design that can be transformed directly into code. It is a template for how one can solve a problem that can be used in numerous different situations.

## Uses of Design Patterns

Design patterns can be used to speed up the development process by offering tested and proven development paradigms. Effective software design necessitates considering problems that might not even become apparent until later in the implementation process. Reusing design patterns helps in preventing subtle issues that can lead to significant issues and improves the overall code readability for coders and architects who are familiar with the patterns.

> Design patterns can be used to speed up the development process by offering tested and proven development paradigms.

Mostly, individuals only understand how to apply specific software design techniques to some problems. All these techniques are complicated to apply to a broader range of issues. Design patterns offer a general solution documented in a format that does not require specifics that are tied to a particular problem.

Additionally, design patterns help developers communicate using well-known and well understood names for software interactions. Some common design patterns can also be improved over time, which makes them all the more robust and better than ad-hoc designs.

## Creational Design Patterns

Creational design patterns are all about the class instantiation. These patterns can be further divided into class creation patterns and object creational patterns. Whilst class creation patterns use inheritance efficiently during the instantiation process, and object creation patterns make use of delegation to get the job done.

## Factory Method

Factory design pattern works as bridge between multiple classes. Consider building a Logger Framework where the log messages maybe written into the log file (represented by FileLogger class) or displayed in the console (represented by ConsoleLogger class). Depending on some logic (for example the variable "logger.logToFile=true" stored in some properties file), an appropriate Logger implementer needs to be used to log messages. The Logger Framework may be used by many different clients, therefor it would be great idea to keep all the logic of creation and instantiation of the objects away from the clients. In this way, the client objects will not have to repeat the same logic again and again and it will be totally isolated from the future changes (like extension of Logger Framework by adding XmlLogger)[15].

### Abstract Factory Method

The advantage of using the abstract method pattern is that you can add additional types to the factory, without much change in the other classes using this class. For example, in your database you can add more types of genders, without affecting the existing code that deals with other genders.

### Builder

One of the most relatable examples of the builder pattern is a restaurant's menu. Assume that you go out for a multi-course dinner to a restaurant. Such a restaurant would have multiple options, for example, appetisers, main course, desserts, beverages and so forth. You would probably choose two or three out of the presented options. A particular client may want to have dinner with the first two options only, leaving out the desserts and beverages option. On the contrary, another would prefer the main course with a glass of fresh lime and dessert, skipping the appetisers

---

[15]Lempert, A. (2019). 10 Design Patterns with real life examples. Medium. Retrieved from: https://medium.com/@analempert/10-design-patterns-with-day-to-day-examples-e4f256d8439

entirely. Similar situations might arise in designing software. You may need to build an object using a subset of the options that are available. Or, you may need to create the object in multiple ways. Using builder pattern will provide a huge amount of flexibility in building objects[16].

**Prototype**

For prototype design pattern the best example is the design of a board game. Let's take an example of chess. Every game of chess has the same initial setup — the king, queen, rook, bishop, knight, and the pawns all have their specific places. Let's say we want to build software to model a chess game. Every time a new Chess game is played, we need to create the initial board layout. Instead of repeating the creation of chessboard each time, we can create an object that contains the initial setup, and clone from it each time a new Chess game is played[17].

**Singleton**

Singleton is a class of which only a single instance can exist.

---

[16]Karanam, R. (2020). Design Patterns for Beginners With Java Examples. DZone. Retrieved from: https://dzone.com/articles/design-patterns-for-beginners-with-java-examples

[17]Karanam, R. (2020). Design Patterns for Beginners With Java Examples. DZone. Retrieved from: https://dzone.com/articles/design-patterns-for-beginners-with-java-examples

## Structural Design Patterns

Structural design patterns comprise of Class and Object composition. Structural class creation patterns use inheritance to compose the interfaces. Structural object patterns define different ways to compose objects to acquire new functionality.

## Adaptor

There are different types of mobile chargers that are not compatible with all kinds of sockets. In such situations, you prefer to carry an adapter that you can use everywhere you go. The same is the case with software designs. When you try to talk to a system that uses a different message format or a language, you need an adapter to translate messages. An interesting example is the communication between a Java program and a web service. Before sending out the data to the service, we need to convert the object into XML or JSON format[18].

## Bridge

The goal of the bridge pattern is to effectively allow for two (or more) levels of abstraction, whereby one category of object (the implementor) can be altered and have no impact on the second category of object (the bridge), which can,

---

[18]Karanam, R. (2020). Design Patterns for Beginners With Java Examples. DZone. Retrieved from: https://dzone.com/articles/design-patterns-for-beginners-with-java-examples

in turn, also be altered and abstracted without impacting the implementor. Many applications and programming frameworks use the bridge pattern to help handle UI/UX components. For example, an object used to define the layout of a component might be abstracted and used in combination with an object used to render the visual output of that same component. By using the bridge pattern and abstracting the layout and the render objects away from one another both can be altered without them impacting one another[19].

**Composite**

There are so many cases where we can use composite design pattern in any programing language. Such as when the data needs to be represented in hierarchy or tree structure, when we need parent-Child relationship, or when parent and child objects need to be treated in same way. A common example can be employee hierarchy in an organization. Manager, CEO and employees all are instances of a Person.

---

[19]Morse, A. (2017). Structural Design Patterns: Bridge. Airbrake. Retrieved from: https://airbrake.io/blog/design-patterns/structural-design-patterns-bridge#:~:text=Many%20applications%20and%20programming%20frameworks,output%20of%20that%20same%20component.

### Decorator

A very good example where the decorator pattern is implemented in Java is the Java I/O packages. This is reflected in the way we create an input stream in an I/O program.

### Façade

Consider the case of a distributed system. You typically have the need for multiple calls across layers. Suppose a system offers the service for online book orders. Whenever an order comes in, several things need to be taken care of, such as checking for the stock, reserving the order, accepting the payment, updating the stock, and generating the invoice. We can create a single facade, such as the order interface, which would manage all incoming orders and provide an interface to the customer. The advantage of using the facade pattern is that it reduces the number of network calls, as well as reduces coupling among classes[20].

---

[20]Karanam, R. (2020). Design Patterns for Beginners With Java Examples. DZone. Retrieved from: https://dzone.com/articles/design-patterns-for-beginners-with-java-examples

## Behavioural Design Patterns

Behavioural design patterns are about Class's objects communication. Behavioural patterns can be described as the patterns that are most precisely concerned with the communication between objects.

### Chain of Responsibility

The best example of this pattern can be seen in the exception handling mechanism of most programming languages. Suppose you have a method1() calling method2(), and method2(), in turn, calls method3(). Assume that method3() throws an exception. If method3() has no exception handling, then the exception is passed on to method2()to handle it. If again method2() has no exception handling inside it, then the exception is passed on to method1(). If even method1() cannot handle it, it gets thrown out of method1() as well[21].

### Command

Consider the scenario when a customer goes to a restaurant and wants to place an order for a meal. The writer merely writes the order he gets on a piece of paper and passes it on to the chef. The chef executes the order and then prepares

[21]Karanam, R. (2020). Design Patterns for Beginners With Java Examples. DZone. Retrieved from: https://dzone.com/articles/design-patterns-for-beginners-with-java-examples

the meal. He passes the piece of paper to the manager. The verbal order from the customer has now become a paper object. This piece of paper is the command object. The command object contains all the details needed to execute the request. Similarly, in object-oriented programming, we can encapsulate all the details of a request into an object and pass that object to execute it. In web applications, when a user types in the details on a form, these details are captured in a single request object, which is then passed across. The interface java.lang.Runnable is also a good example of how this pattern is implemented. We create threads in Java by extending the Runnable interface, which has all the logic for execution in its start() method. When we want to create and start a thread, we pass this class to the start() method[22].

**Interpreter**

One of the best examples of interpreter design pattern is Google Translator. Google Translator Application offers a Web interface, Mobile app and ios app and a software-enabled API. Google Translate supports more than 100 languages at different levels. We can offer input in every language in the Google Translator, then what the Google

[22]Karanam, R. (2020). Design Patterns for Beginners With Java Examples. DZone. Retrieved from: https://dzone.com/articles/design-patterns-for-beginners-with-java-examples

Translator does it reads the data and it will provide the output in a different language[23].

**Strategy**

The Strategy encapsulates an algorithm inside a class. The strategy pattern is suitable for

- An application that should be able to choose a sorting algorithm at runtime (Bubble sort, Quick-Sort and so on).

- Implementing the shopping site: the user adds items to the basket and by the end on check-out, the user can choose the payment strategy in runtime: PayPal, Credit Card and so on.

- A game where we can have different characters and each character can have multiple weapons to attack but at a time can use only one weapon.

---

[23]Java Code Geeks. (2020). Java Interpreter Design Pattern Example. Website. Retrieved from: https://examples.javacodegeeks.com/core-java/java-interpreter-design-pattern-example/#:~:text=Google%20Translator%20is%20a%20really,output%20in%20a%20different%20language.

The method attack() will have different implementation depends on which weapon is being used.

- Client that may need to apply a different compression algorithms[24].

**Visitor**

The Visitor defines a new operation to a class without any change. The Visitor pattern represents an operation to be performed on the elements of an object structure without changing the classes on which it operates. This pattern can be observed in the operation of a taxi company. When a person calls a taxi company (accepting a visitor), the company dispatches a cab to the customer. Upon entering the taxi the customer, or Visitor, is no longer in control of his or her own transportation, the taxi (driver) is[25].

---

[24]Lempert, A. (2019). 10 Design Patterns with real life examples. Medium. Retrieved from: https://medium.com/@analempert/10-design-patterns-with-day-to-day-examples-e4f256d8439

[25]Source Making. (2020). Visitor Design Pattern. Website. Retrieved from: https://sourcemaking.com/design_patterns/visitor#:~:text=The%20Visitor%20pattern%20represents%20an,a%20cab%20to%20the%20customer.

# OVERVIEW OF MODERN CONCURRENCY AND PARALLELISM CONCEPTS

# Overview of Modern Concurrency and Parallelism Concepts

Most software engineers know about operating system (OS) level processes and threads. They are taught in all university OS courses. However, newer concepts promising higher throughput, less overhead, latency, and development efforts have emerged. I was perplexed as I couldn't find a succinct and systematic description and comparison. This is precisely the goal of this chapter – to summarise, exemplify and compare terms like green threads, fibres, goroutine, actors etc.

## Concurrency vs. Parallelism

Let's start by clarifying two important concepts – concurrency and parallelism. Until recently I considered them synonymous and there is still some ambiguity in the community about what they mean. According to Rob Pike's talk, concurrency is about composing independent processes (in the general meaning of the term process) to work together, while parallelism is about actually executing multiple processes simultaneously. Concurrency is about the design and structure of the application, while parallelism is about the actual execution. Naturally, the terms are related.

In order to achieve efficient utilisation of a multi-core system (i.e. good parallelism) you need scalable and flexible design with no bottlenecks (i.e. good concurrency).

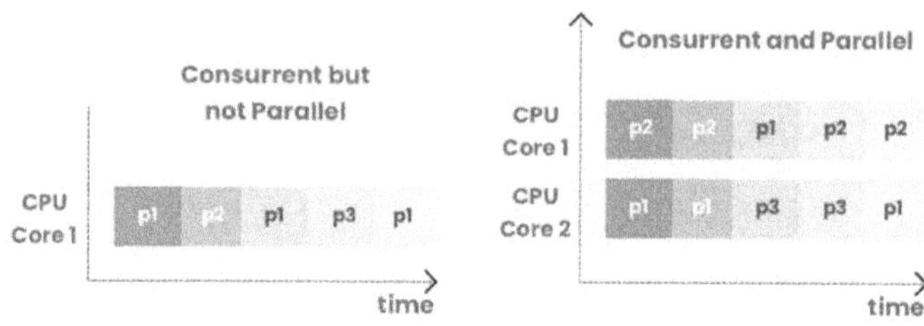


**Figure 6.1**

**Concurrent vs. Parallel**

Let's take a multi-threaded application as an example. The separation of the application into threads defines its concurrent model. The mapping of these threads on the available cores defines its level or parallelism. A concurrent system may run efficiently on a single processor, in which case it is not parallel. We can have it vice versa as well. It is possible to have parallelism without concurrency. For example, in SIMD architectures there are simultaneous/parallel computations, although only one instruction is run at a time.

## Processes and Threads

If you know about OS processes and threads you may wish to skip this section. A process is an instance of a program being executed. Each process has its own address space, which cannot be accessed from other processes. Hence, processes are isolated from each other and cannot directly access each other's memory, which increases security and fault tolerance. Special inter-process communication techniques like sockets and pipelines can be used to communicate between processes. The OS preemtively schedules the processes' access to CPU resources.

OS processes can be expensive to create, as each one has its own address space, program code, open file handles etc. Furthermore, the inter-process communication can be inefficient and cumbersome to program. Enter threads (a.k.a. lightweight processes). A thread is a separate line of execution (i.e. a sequence of instructions) within a process. A process can have multiple threads, all of which share its address space, file handles etc. Starting a thread is cheaper, as fewer resources need to be allocated. The threads within a process are concurrent and can execute in parallel. Each thread maintains its own programming stack. Alike processes, the OS scheduler preemptively schedules all threads.

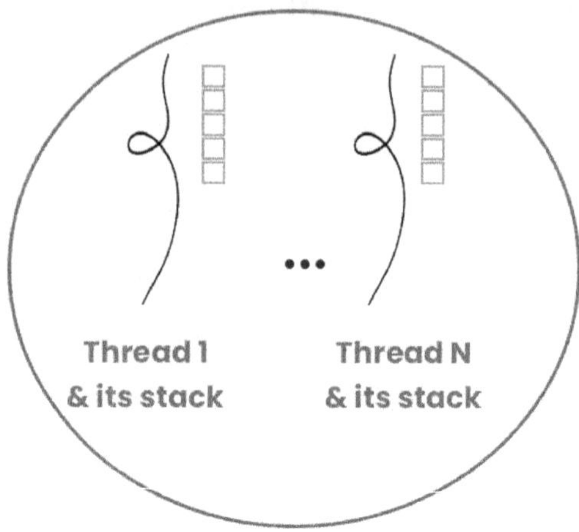


**Figure 6.2**

***Each thread in a process has its own stack***

Since all threads within a process share the same address space, they can communicate much more easily. However, this makes multi-threaded programming notoriously difficult, as the access to shared variables must be carefully synchronised. Acquiring and releasing locks can significantly slow down an application as threads can be blocked for long time periods. Furthermore, blocking leads to context switching, which is expensive.

Another problem is that each thread has its own stack (typically ~2MB). This limits the number of threads you can have in a system to at most tens of thousands of threads for machines with large RAM. In a web server running a separate thread per client, this will limit the number of clients you can serve, although most of the threads may be idle (e.g. waiting on I/O). Thread pools and queues can be used to resolve the issue and to avoid excessive thread allocation. This may result in further contention, as the access to the pool itself must be synchronised and the number of incoming requests may be greater than the pool size, which is still limited by the maximum number of threads in the system.

## Green Threads

When Java was introduced 20 years ago it featured threads as a core concept and aimed to run on all platforms. At that point some platforms (e.g. old Solaris systems) did not have native support for threads and the JVM could not map its threads to OS threads. Hence, they had to emulate threads on top of such platforms. Such threads are called Green Threads. Green threads run in user space, and are scheduled by a library or a virtual machine (VM). Thus, the OS kernel "sees" green threads as belonging to the same process and cannot schedule them on multiple cores simuateneosly! Therefore, green threads are a concurrency concept, but not a parallel one. Java has effectively abandoned green threads in favour of mapping to native OS threads.

## Protothreads

Protothreads are defined as stackless threads. All protothreads share the same stack and context switching is done by “stack rewinding”. They are not preemptable, and only switch context when a blocking operation is invoked. As there is no stack, all local variables are not preserved upon a context switch! Protothreads are available only as a C library, and are used for low-memory embedded devices. Documentation is not too much, except for some academic papers and a presentation. As they run on a single stack, I assume protothreads are concurrent but not truly parallel. Protothreads seem to be a programming abstraction for event driven programming, rather than a true parallelism enabler.

## Fibers

Remember that threads are lightweight processes. Well, Fibers are lightweight threads :). Fibers implement user space co-operative multitasking, rather than kernel level preemptive one. Thus, a fiber cannot be forcefully pre-empted by the OS kernel. A fiber must voluntarily yield its execution to allow another one to run. Fibers always start and stop/yield in a number of predefined places. This makes programming easier, as the programmers are guaranteed that their code will not be abruptly interrupted and its data structures accessed by another fiber. However, fibers must play nice and yield now and then to allow concurrency – this cannot be delegated to the OS kernel. Fibers do have their own stacks, but the fiber switching is done in user space by the execution environment, not the OS kernel generic scheduler. Yielding and resuming are respectively performed by saving and restoring the fiber's execution context/stack also more generally known as continuation. Fibers have small stacks stored and managed in user space. These factors should significantly improve their performance compared to threads. Fibers are a concurrency concept, but are not truly parallel. Typically, each fiber has a parent thread, just as each thread belongs to a process. Multiple fibers from the same thread cannot run simultaneously. In other words, multiple execution paths can coexists in the form of fibers (i.e. concurrency) but they cannot actually run at the same time (parallelism).

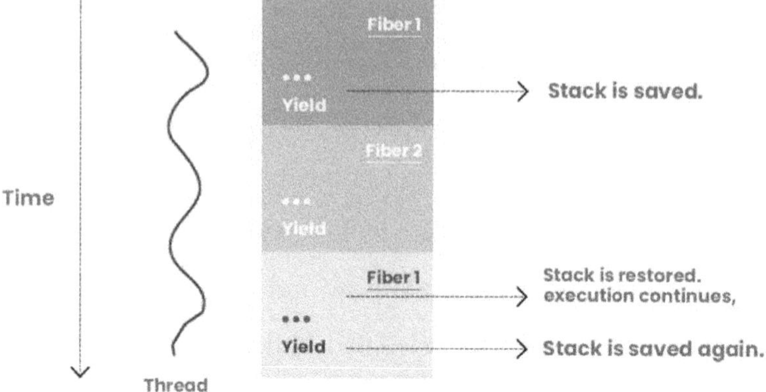


**Figure 6.3**

***Multiple Fibers in a thread***

Fibers are usually short-lived tasks, unlike threads which are usually long lived. Hence, fibers can have smaller stacks. For instance, the Quasar library allows you to specify the stack size of new fibres. Hence, you can have much more fibers (i.e. millions) than threads (thousands). There are a lot of articles online about the Quasar library, which supports fibers in Java. In my opinion Quasar fibers are not true fibers as per the above definition, and look more like goroutines, as they can achieve true parallelism and communicate via channels. They are more flexible, but not the same :). So let's give an example of fibers in Ruby. The following example defines a Fiber, which generates the Fibonacci numbers and is a modified version of the InfoQ example. After each number is generated, the fiber yields. Once it is resumed, the fiber reinstates its stack, generates another number and yields again.

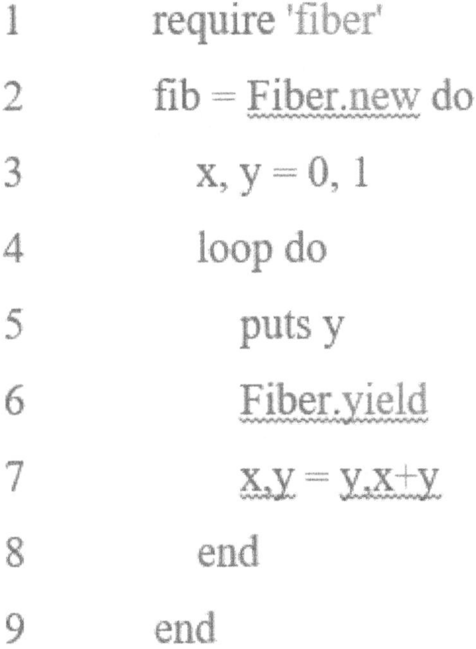

```
require 'fiber'
fib = Fiber.new do
   x, y = 0, 1
   loop do
      puts y
      Fiber.yield
      x,y = y,x+y
   end
end
```

It is responsibility of the caller to start and resume the fibers. The following lines print the first 20 Fibonacci numbers.

```
20.times { fib.resume }
```

Computing Fibonacci is not the most impressive or useful example. Indeed, there is a much better use case. Let's assume we have a wrapper of a native async library for downloading HTTP resources. The methods of this library can be provided with callbacks, which are executed once the async operation completes. In this scenario, the fiber can start an asynchronous HTTP operation and the yield. As a callback, we can provide an expression which resumes the fiber.

So we can have a fiber yield, while an external native library is doing extensive I/O, and then resume once this is done. Upon resuming the fiber can for example update the user interface (UI). This happens on the same thread! The alternative would be to start a separate thread for the I/O task, which blocks until it is complete and then concurrently modifies the UI.

For an example of how to use Fibers in Ruby in such situation, you can check out this article. In fact this approach of wrapping a long running backround task in a fiber is so widesperead, that C# introduces a specialised Async/Await language structure for it. As I mentioned, there is still some ambiguity in regard to many concurrency terms. For example, in Quasar fibers can run in parallel. GHC and Mercury can migrate fibers from one thread to another, and GHC can even preempt them. In this section, I've use the Wikipedia definition of Fiber, but other definitions exists as well.

## Generators

As a step towards coroutines, we will discuss generators, also known as semicoroutines. You're probably familiar with this concept if you've studied python or a functional language like Lisp. Most programming languages have the concept of subroutines in the form of procedures, functions, or methods. When called, a typical subroutine completes at once and returns a single value. It does not hold any state between invocations.

From the client code, a generator looks like a normal subroutine – it can be invoked and will return a value. However, a generator yields (rather than return!) a value and preserves its state – i.e. the values of the local variables. Again, this is known as continuation. When this generator is called again, its state is restored and the execution continues from the point of the last yielding until a new yield is encountered. Subroutines can be thought of as generators which never yield. The following example demonstrates a python 2 generator, which consequently produces numbers greater than n.

```
def countfrom(n):
while True:
yield n
n += 1
```

The following invocations demonstrate how generators work. Note that in python 2, the next method is used to call a generator.

```
# Create a generator
g = countfrom(5)
# Prints 5
print (g.next())
# Prints 6
print (g.next())
```

The first invocation of the generator reaches the yield statement, saves the local variable state (n=5) and yields its value. The second invocation restores the local variable (n=5), continues the execution after the yield statement and hence increases n to 6. When yield is reached again, the local variable state (n=6) is saved again and yielded to the caller. Perhaps you can see a lot similarity between generators and fibers. Indeed, they are almost equivalent concepts. When a generator reaches a yield statement it saves its state and allows other code to execute. The same thing happens with a fiber, which saves its stack and lets another fiber run. When a generator is called, it restores its state and executes until a yield statement is encountered again. The same happens with a fiber, which once it is resumed runs uninterupted until it voluntarily yields.

## Coroutines

Using a fiber library can be cumbersome, and thus some programming languages introduce coroutines. The two concepts are functionally equivalent. However, coroutines are implemented with specific syntax on the programming language level. Coroutines are a generalisation of generators. When you are invoking a generator, you can not specify a parameter - i.e. in the previoous example we could not write g.next(7). Coroutines allow for this. When the coroutine is resumed, the specified value is provided to it in the form of a result of yield. The following example illustrates this:

```
def countfrom(n):
while True:
 i = yield n
 n += i
```

This code can be invoked as:

```
# Create the coroutine
g = countfrom(5)
# First call to the coroutine – Prints 5
print(g.next())
# Prints 7
print(g.send(2))
# Prints 10
print(g.send(3))
```

In Python 2 there are some syntactic specifics. When you call a coroutine for the first time, you have to use next, just like with generators. Subsequent calls must use the send method, providing the actual value. This is needed, because in the beginning the coroutine is not halted/paused on a yield statement. The invocation of next intialises it to such a state. Subsequent invocations of send actually illustrate the invocation of the coroutine. Philosophically speaking, subroutines and coroutines are two different ways to structure a program. With subroutines, you're dividing the program into subparts which execute to completion one after another.

With coroutines, you divide your programs into collegial parts, whose lifecycles overlap, and which exchange messages by yielding to each other. If that was a bit too abstract, you may want to consult Berkley's lectures for more details. More details on Python generators and coroutines can be found in David Beazley's presentation. Remember that coroutines are not truly parallel. The same is true for generators and fibers. You can still avoid CPU blocking if you start some native asynchronous I/O and then yield, but you cannot use multiple CPU cores simultaneously.

## Goroutines

The Go programming language introduces the concept of Goroutines. They have been described as coroutines which can run in parallel. In terms of implementation, the Go runtime environment maintains an internal pool of native OS threads. Each goroutine is assigned to a thread from this pool which executes its logic. Once a goroutine blocks (e.g. for I/O) the runtime environment can use its thread for another goroutine. When a routine resumes, there is no guarantee that it will be scheduled on the same thread.

Each goroutine's logic is in fact defined in a function. The Go runtime acts as a mediator which schedules these functions on the underlying thread pool. In some special cases, a long running goroutine can be preemted and its thread given to another routine. Otherwise, the assignment of goroutines to threads is not preemptable. The overall goal is to minimise the time threads are blocked, and thus serve the application with fewer threads and context switches.

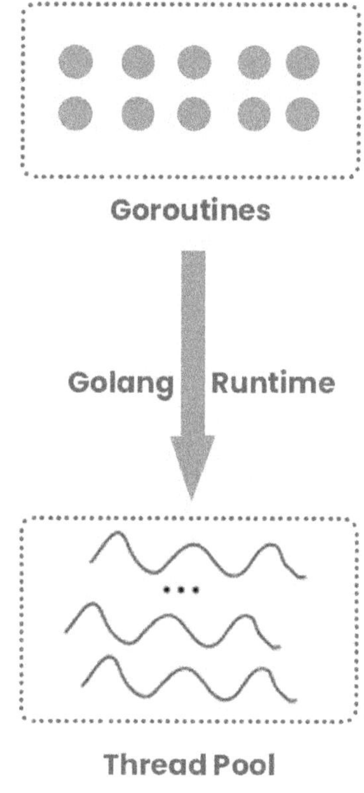


**Figure 6.4**

Goroutines communicate with each other via channels, similarly to processes communication. This alleviates the synchronisation issues of shared memory communication that threads have. This also bears some resemblance with how coroutines communicate by yielding values to each other.

## Actors

Alike the Object-Oriented Model, the Actor Model is a way to model computation. Originally developed in the 70s, the actor model is in fact rather simple. It introduces a single concept (the actor) which has a few basic properties.

So what is an Actor? According to the overview by Hewit et al. an actor has the following properties:

1. Processing – an actor can do computation;
2. Storage – an actor can maintain state, similar to a Java object;
3. Communication – an actor can receive and send messages from and to other actors.

In the actor model, a system is represented as a set of actors which exchange messages. When an actor receives a message, it can do one or few of the following:

1. Send messages to other actors;
2. Create new actors;
3. Change its state – this new state will be used for processing the future message.

A single actor is inherently non-concurrent (i.e. single threaded) and you need not worry about synchronising the access to its state. However, implementations of this model can run an actor's logic in parallel if it is stateless/immutable – i.e. it does not use the last option of the above list. If an actor is stateful the implementation may choose to do some queuing. Either way, at a conceptual level you can think of actors as running one message at a time.

When an actor sends a message, it does not wait for confirmation or response (think UDP not TCP). Also, there are no guarantees about the order of message arrivals or delays. Hence, actors communicate in a completely asynchronous and distributed fashion. Moreover, actors are the atomic components in this model, share no state and are themselves non-concurrent thus removing the need for locks and synchronisation. Once you've built an actor model, it is inherently concurrent. You can deploy on multiple cores and even networked machines to achieve true parallelism.

As a practical example of an Actor-based framework we can consider Akka - one of the most prominent implementations targeted at the JVM. In Akka actors are arranged in a hierarchy. Each actor is identified with its path from the root. Every parent actor is designated as a supervisor of its child actors. An actor can implement its own supervisor strategy, which gets executed when supervised actors fails. Typically, this is used for restarting or recreating failed actors.

Under the hood, Akka uses a thread pool. Based on the configuration and the message dispatchers (classes forwarding messages to actors), Akka schedules the actors on the available threads. Actors can also be replicated and put behind a Dispatcher which load balances the incoming messages among them. This can increase availability and responsiveness. Finally, actors can be transparently distributed on multiple machines or a cluster.

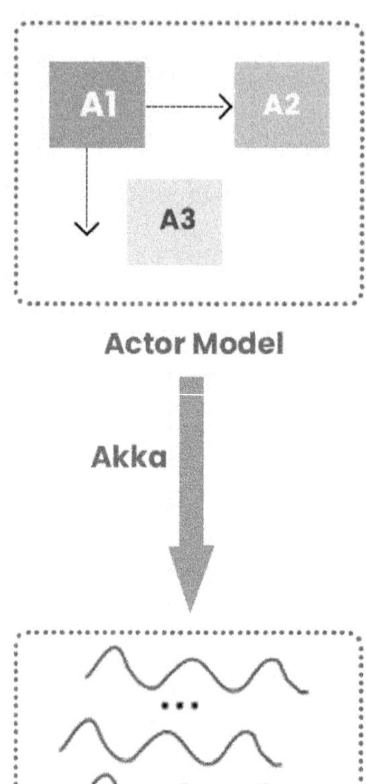


**Figure 6.5**

***Actors***

## LMAX Disruptor

The LMAX Disruptor method is a way to implement producer-consumer systems more efficiently. It has been implemented as a Java library, but the approach can be applied in non-JVM environments. While actors, goroutines, and fibers propose efficient concurrent models "on top" of threads, the Disruptor library embraces the multi-threaded approach and tries to improve it. It does so by preallocating memory, avoiding excessive locks and utilising modern processors' capabilities.

The library creators argue that locking data between threads is the main culprit for system latency. To a certain extent this has been mitigated by the Compare and Swap (CAS) capability of modern processors, allowing a piece of memory to be conditionally written in a single atomic instruction. This is how most java.util.concurrent atomic types work under the hood. Even with CAS, locking seems to be a performance bottleneck, as the CPU internally must lock its instructions pipeline.

Another major problem of the producer-consumer systems is the dynamic nature of queues, which are used to store data in a producer-consumer approach. Such queues can usually grow and shrink dynamically resulting in runtime memory allocation and garbage collection.

This can significantly degrade performance. Furthermore, most queues are implemented as linked lists, and thus occupy non-adjacent memory addresses. This hinders the memory locality of CPU operations and can lead to many cache misses. Hence, the Disruptor library preallocates a static array of memory, which it uses throughout the execution.

The data structure they use is a ring buffer, which is implemented as an array. The elements/objects of this array are preallocated. To achieve the ring effect, the remainders of all indices are used. Let's assume there is a single producer. There will be a single index within the ring buffer designating the lastly written element. Once the producer creates/produces an input entry, the corresponding buffer entry will be updated and the counter incremented.

That update should be "in-place" to avoid creating garbage. Each consumer maintains its own index designating the last read item. It waits until that index precedes the index of the producer and then can consume all newly produced elements. Waiting can be done in multiple ways – e.g. periodically polling. When multiple producers are involved,

LMAX Disruptor can use CAS locking to determine the value of the producer index for each of them.

Using this approach we can avoid locking in most circumstances and we only use a preallocated fixed size data structure. However, if the producer significantly outpaces the consumers the buffer won't be enough. Hence, it's a good idea to preallocate huge buffers of thousands or even millions of elements.

This will allow the consumers to catch up with a producer which suddently spikes in demand. If the consumers can't catch up given such a huge buffer, then such computation would not be viable with any other queuing model as well – the only solution would be to improve the throughput of the consumers.

Apart from simple producer-consumer systems, the LMAX Disruptor can also increase the performance of pipeline or workflow systems. As one node is continuously producing/streaming data, the dependent nodes can consume it in real time with minimal latency.

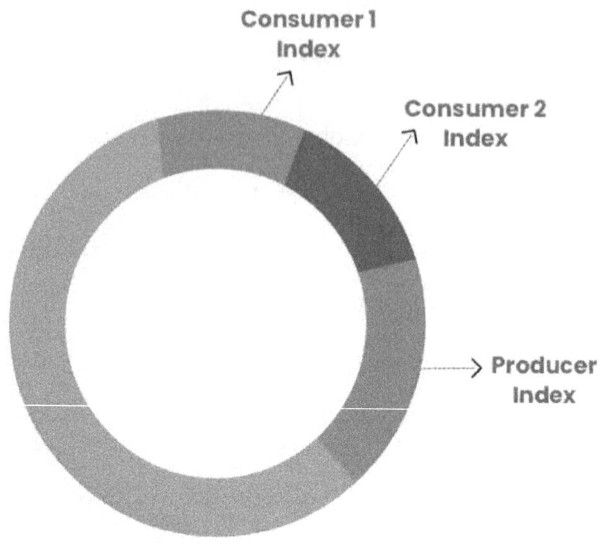


**Figure 6.6**

***LMAX Disruptor***

# COMMON SOFTWARE ARCHITECTURAL PATTERNS

# Common Software Architectural Patterns

Have you ever wondered how large-scale enterprise structures are designed? Before significant software development begins, we need to select an acceptable architecture that can provide us with the necessary features and quality attributes. You should therefore consider the various architectures before implementing them to your design.

## What is an Architectural Pattern?

As per the definition by Wikipedia,

"An architectural pattern is a general, reusable solution to a commonly occurring problem in software architecture within a given context. Architectural patterns are similar to software design pattern but have a broader scope."

In this chapter, I will briefly explain the ten common architectural patterns along with their use, pros and cons.

## Layered Pattern

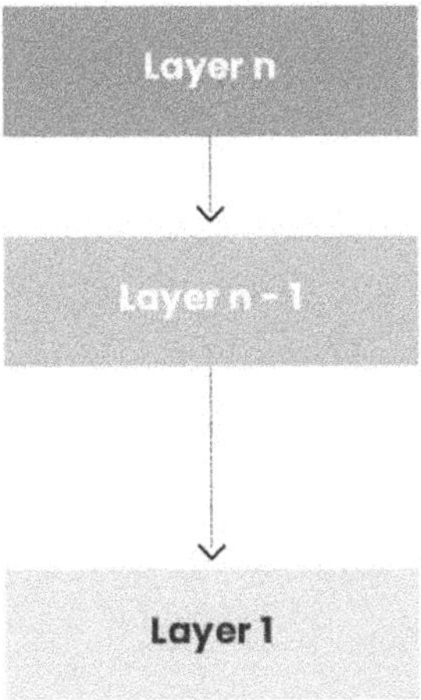


**Figure 7.1**

***Layered Pattern***

This pattern can be used to organise programs that can be divided into groups of sub tasks, each of which is at a different abstraction level. Each layer offers services for the next upper layer.

**The Most Commonly Found 4 Layers Of A General Information System**

1. Presentation layer (also known as UI layer)

2. Application layer (also known as service layer)

3. Business logic layer (also known as domain layer)

4. Data access layer (also known as persistence layer)

**Usage**

1. General desktop applications.

2. E commerce web applications.

## Client-Server Pattern

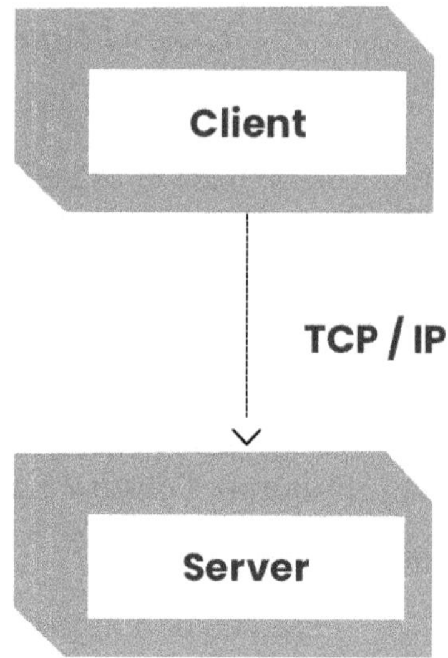


**Figure 7.2**

**Client Server Pattern**

This pattern is made up of two parties; a server as well as several clients. The server portion offers services to several client constituents. Customers request services from the server, and the server delivers the necessary services to those customers. In addition, the server tends to respond to customer request.

**Usage**

Can be used in online applications for example email, document sharing and banking.

## Master-Slave Pattern

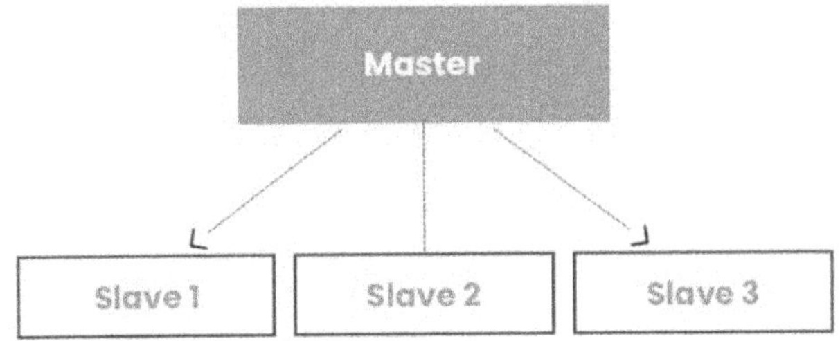


**Figure 7.3**

**Master Slave Pattern**

This pattern consists of two parts: the master and the slave. The master component assigns jobs to the same slave constituents and calculates the final outcome of the return of the slaves. This pattern is quite common in database management system (DBMS).

**Usage**

1. In the case of database replication, the primary database is considered to be a primary source, and the slave databases are related to it.

2. Peripherals link to the bus on the operating network (master and slave drives).

## Pipe-Filter Pattern

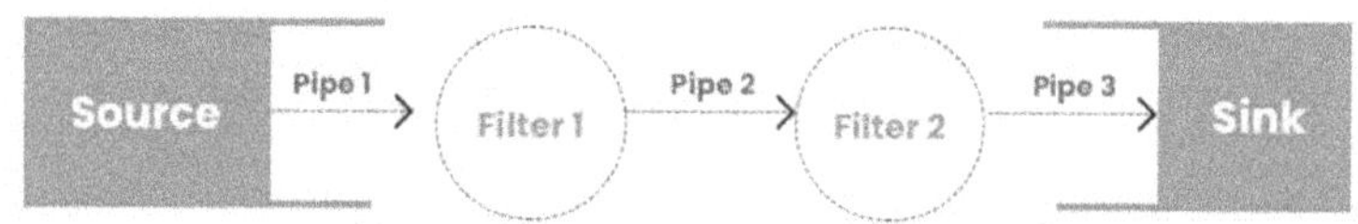


**Figure 7.4**

**Pipe Filter Pattern**

This pattern can be used to create systems that generate and process data streams. Each processing stage is embedded in the filter segment. The data to be processed is passed through the pipeline. Such pipes can be used for buffering or synchronization purposes.

**Usage**

1. Compilers. Successive filters perform lexical analysis, sorting, semantic analysis, and code generation.

2. Bioinformatics workflows.

## Broker Pattern

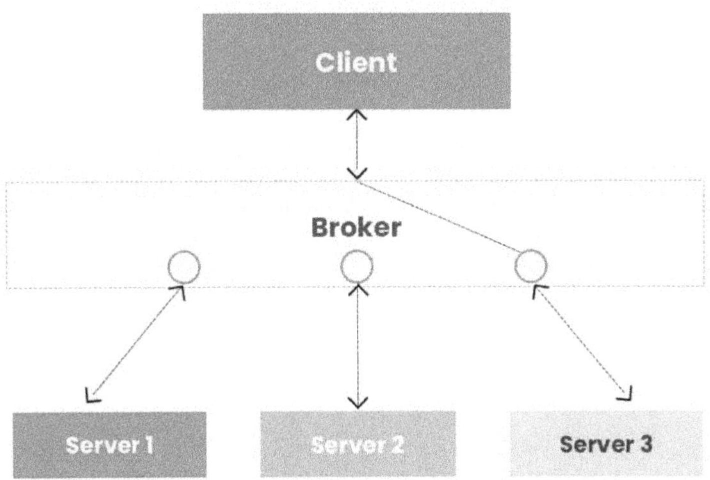


**Figure 7.5**

**Broker Pattern**

This pattern is used for the structure of distributed systems with differentiated components. Such modules can communicate with each other through remote service invocations. The broker function is responsible for organizing the contact between the components.

The servers publish their capabilities (services and features) to the broker. Customers order a service from the broker, and the broker then refers the customer to an acceptable service from his list.

**Usage**

Usage can be used to message broker software such as Apache ActiveMQ, Apache Kafka, RabbitMQ and JBoss Messaging.

## Peer-to-Peer Pattern

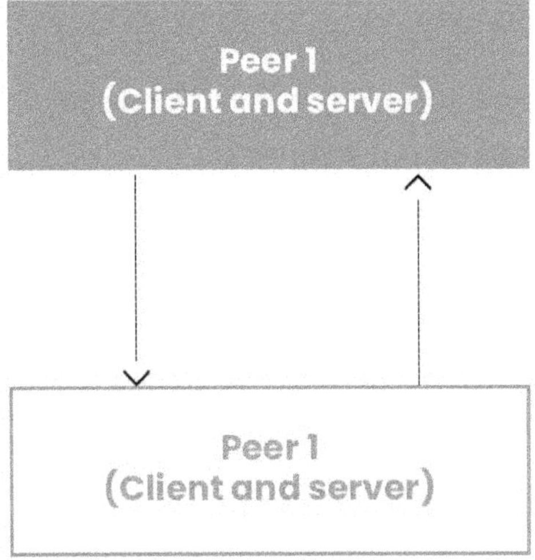


**Figure 7.6**

**Peer to Peer Pattern**

Within this system, individual components are referred to as peers. Peers that act both as a client, requiring service from other peers, and as a server, providing services to other peers. A peer might act as a consumer or as a server or both, and might even change its function dynamically over time.

**Usage**

1. File sharing networks for instance Gnutella and G2)

2. Multimedia protocols for instance P2PTV and PDTP.

## Event-Bus Pattern

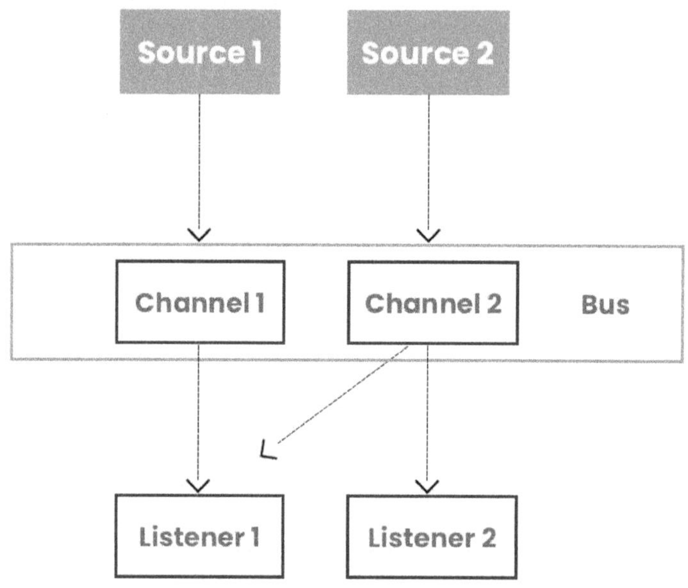


**Figure 7.7**

**Event Bus Pattern**

The pattern deals specifically with events and has four main components: event source, event listener, channel and event bus. Sources post messages to different networks on the case bus. Listeners are subscribed to specific channels. Listeners are informed of messages that are released on a channel they have already subscribed to.

**Usage**

1. Android development
2. Notification services

## Model-View-Controller Pattern

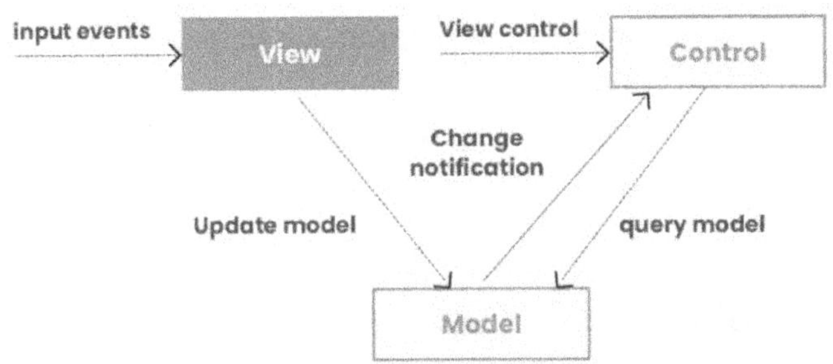


**Figure 7.8**

**Model View Controller Pattern**

This pattern, also identified as the MVC pattern, divides the interactive framework into three parts,

1. model — contains the core functionality and data
2. view — displays the information to the user (more than one view may be defined)
3. controller — handles the input from the user

It is done to distinguish internal representations of information from the way information is interpreted to and approved by the user. It decouples the components and makes efficient re-use of the code.

**Usage**

1. Architecture of World Wide Web software in major programming languages.

2. Application systems include Django and Rails.

## Blackboard Pattern

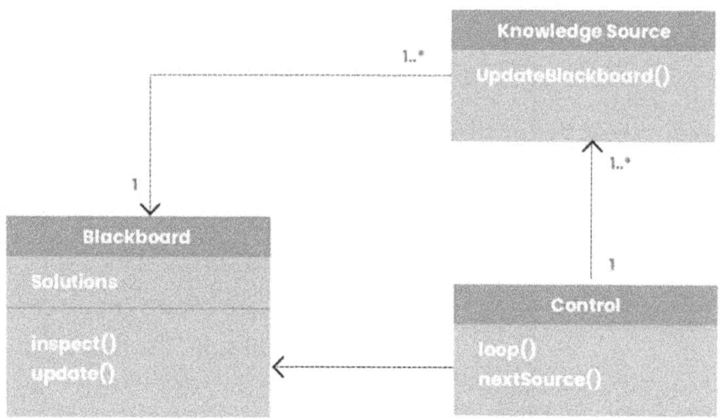


**Figure 7.9**

**Blackboard Pattern**

This approach is useful for problems for which a deterministic solution technique is not known. The blackboard design consists of three major parts.

1. Blackboard — a standardised global memory containing space solution objects.

2. Knowledge source — Specialised modules with their own representation;

3. Control component — choose, customise, and execute modules.

Many of the components have access to the blackboard. Components can generate new data objects that are added to the blackboard. Components are searching for different types of data on the blackboard, which can be identified by pattern matching the current information source.

**Usage**

1. Speech recognition
2. Vehicle identification and tracking
3. Protein structure identification
4. Sonar signals interpretation.

## Interpreter Pattern

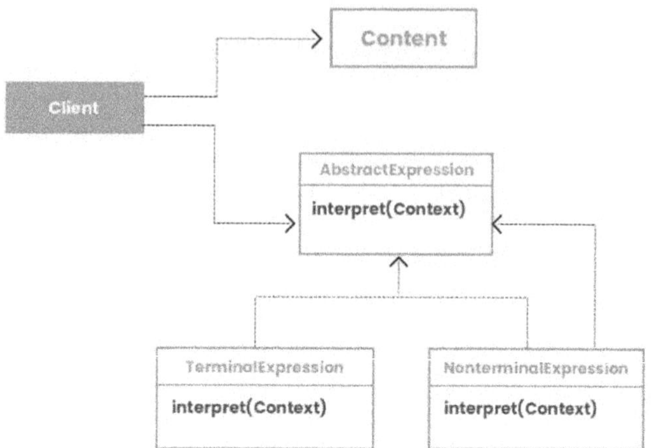


**Figure 7.10**

**Interpreter Pattern**

This pattern is used to construct a component that interprets programs written in a particular language. This also determines how to interpret program lines, known as phrases or phrases written in a particular language. The basic principle is to assign every language symbol a class.

**Usage**

1. Database query languages such as SQL.

2. Languages used to describe communication protocols.

# AUTHENTICATION AND AUTHORIZATION

# Authentication and Authorization

One of the essential considerations for a designer while designing a web app is developing a user security model. Security model is essential to protect a web application from security threats and malicious traffic that can manipulate vulnerabilities in an application's code. In context of security, the two most commonly used terms are Authentication and Authorization. A majority of people assume that the two terms are interchangeable and convey the same meaning. However, this is not true. The two terms may sound similar but have entirely different meaning and functions.

**Figure 8.1**

## Authentication

When a user tries to access an application, they first have to verify their identity. This verification is known as authentication. An exclusive identifier is linked with a user which is the username or user id. When we talk about basic security, a combination of username and password is used to authenticate a user. Such authentication is also called local authentication. In Addition to local authentication, there are several other advanced authentication methods such as Two factor authentication and multifactor authentication.

## Local Authentication

Local authentication is the most common technique. its process is as follows:

- The user signs up for an application using an identifier such as user name, email, phone number
- The application saves user information in its database
- The application sends a verification email/message to the user to confirm the registration;

- After successful confirmation, user logs in to the application
- On successful authentication, the user is allowed access to specific resources

**Two Factor Authentication**

Two-factor authentication is also commonly known as two-step verification or dual-factor authentication. It is a security technique in which users are required to provide two different authentication factors to verify themselves. This purpose of this authentication method is to ensure better security for user as well as application resources.

> Two-factor authentication is also commonly known as two-step verification or dual-factor authentication.

Two-factor authentication provides an advanced level of security compared to local authentication. In two-step authentication, a user has to provide a second security factor along with a password or pin code. The purpose of this second factor is to add an additional layer of security to the authentication process. It protects the user account from being accessed by attackers. Because knowing just victim's password is not enough to gain an authorised access to the account.

The second factor required in two-step authentication process can be:

**A knowledge Factor**

This is something the user knows. For example, a password, pin code or the answer of a security question.

**A possession Factor**

This is something the user owns. For example, an ID card, phone number, email id or a smart device to approve authentication requests.

**An inherence Factor**

This is something as user is. It is also called a biometric factor. It includes finger id, face or voice recognition.

### A location Factor

This denotes the area from which the authentication request is being made. With this factor, as user is only allowed to access an account if they are within a specific geolocation or source IP range.

### Multi Factor Authentication

Just like two-step verification, multi factor authentication also works on the same technique. However, it may require a user to provide more than two authentication factors.

## Authorization

When a user has successfully completed the authentication process, the next step is authorization process. Authorization refers to what a user is allowed to do and see on your website or server. The permission is granted to users according to their level.

---

Authorization refers to what a user is allowed to do and see on your website or server.

---

Let's understand this with an example of blogging platforms. When a blog writer creates a post, it is openly available to read. So, every user can access it without having to go through authentication process.

However, if a user wants to create a post, they must sign up in the blogging platform as an author. Similarly, to publish and edit that post, a user must have editor and administrator privileges. Authorization rules are necessary to maintain the transparency of an application usage. Another simple example of authorization is Facebook pages and group. The founder of the group or page can give customised access to specific people according to their role. These roles include editor, moderator and admin.

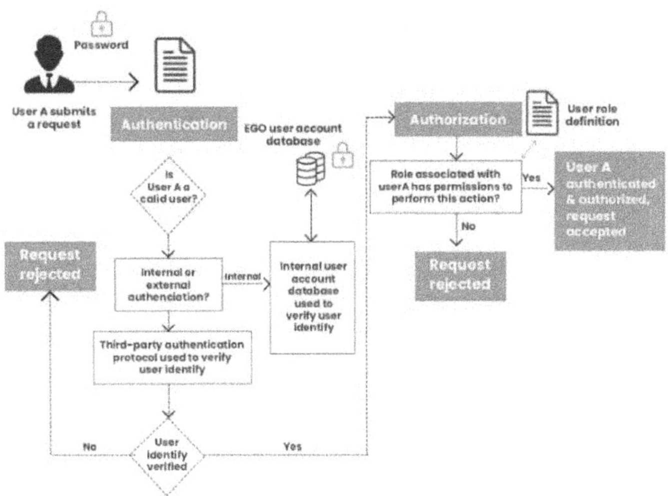


**Figure 8.2**

The higher the user role is, the more resources they are allowed to access. Similarly, there are different websites that offer free and premium services. The users who want to benefit from free features have limited permissions. However, premium users can enjoy a variety of other features also.

## Access Control

Once is it is identified who the user is and what resources they can access, it is necessary to practice a regular control to prevent the user from accessing those resources they are not supposed to. This is referred to as access control mechanism. The primary types of access control are

- Discretionary Access Control (DAC)
- Role-Based Access Control (RBAC)
- Attribute-Based Access Control (ABAC)
- Mandatory Access Control (MAC)

### Discretionary Access Control

As the name signifies, the administrator of the application or resource has the right to grant permission to anyone based on their discretion. The owner of the information typically makes access decision based on the credentials of the user that they provided at the time of authentication. Such controls are easy to administer because they are entirely owner controlled. However, with such control, some users are granted more accesses and privileges than are needed.

**Role-Based Access Control**

In RBAC, accesses and privileges are granted according to the role of a user. A common example of RBAC is an HR system where each employee is allowed to access resources according to their job role and designation only. This type of control is very affective because it aligns with security principles like segregation of duties and least privileges.

**Attribute-Based Access Control**

ABAC can be referred to as a sub category of Role-Based Access Control. In ABAC, the control is more filtered. For example, in RBAC, every employee is allowed to access attendance board. However, only those employees who are in HR department have the permission to edit the attendance board.

**Mandatory Access Control**

Mandatory Access Control is centrally controlled system which protects the resources by assigning sensitivity tags on information and linking this to the level of sensitivity a user is performing at. Unlike DAC, the owner or administrator of the resource has not right to modify and delegate the control based on their discretion. MAC is usually suitable for highly sensitive resources, including multilevel secure military applications or mission-critical data applications.

# EVENTS AND EVENTS PROCESSING

# Events and Events Processing

We are currently living in a world of information that revolves around a plethora of information flows and data on the Internet. Understanding this information is becoming increasingly complex. Therefore, we need to find effective ways to make the best use of this data and improve the quality of available information. Event processing system is one of the best ways to achieve this purpose. However, before getting into the details of event processing, we first need to understand what an event is.

## What are Events?

An event, in terms of computer, is an action or happening that can be recognised by a program. An event can be user-generated. Keystrokes and mouse clicks are examples of user-generated events. An event can also be system-generated. For example, when your computer notifies you when a program is loading or your system is running out of memory. An event-driven program is designed to identify events the moment they happen, and then handle them using some event-handling procedure.

Keystrokes and mouse clicks are examples of user-generated events.

The common examples of events are:

- Receiving an HTML message on a web server
- Pressing a key in a text editor
- Approval or rejection of a loan application
- Detection of illegal activity in a bank's information system.

## Event Programming

Event programming is a technique that is applied during the development stage of a product. Basically, it separates event-processing logic from the rest of a program's code. Event-driven applications can be designed in any programming language. Most of the object-oriented and visual languages are compliant with event-driven programming, including Visual Basic, Visual C++ and Java.

In an event-driven application, the main loop listens to the events, and once an event is detected, it triggers a call-back function. In this way, in an event-driven program, the flow of the information is guided by events such as user actions (mouse clicks, key presses), sensor outputs, or messages from other programs or threads. Event-driven programming is used broadly in graphical user interfaces and applications that execute actions in response to user input such as JavaScript web applications.

For software designers, creating an event-driven application is quite complex in terms of design and delivery. This is because conventional applications are based on request-driven technique instead of event-driven interactions. Request-driven applications work differently. In such applications, the customer directs the interactions, commanding which service will process the request. The customer must then wait for a response to the request. On the contrary, event-driven programs allow different parts of the system to respond to events as they're received, and multiple services to process events at the same time. The system components that perform this action can be either simple services or very complex systems. Their role is to generate events and trigger actions.

> For software designers, creating an event-driven application is quite complex in terms of design and delivery.

Once the actions have been triggered, it now depends on the communications and intermediation middleware (i.e. an intermediary layer) to control the delivery of event notifications and act as an event broker. However, event-driven programs may need some traditional request-driven design to be built in, as they can integrate and improve one another, depending on the type of business process being applied. The request-driven method, for example, allows better control of action through its command-driven and structured technique. In contrast, the event-driven model provides better flexibility, supporting real-time, business-driven events. Both approaches currently have some limitations. The request-driven method is relatively inflexible, while the event-driven model lacks end-to-end consistency because of the need for that intermediary layer.

## Complex Event Processing

In simple event processing, the events are responded to one by one. However, complex event processing (CEP) is a method which works by taking action on a series of data points that arise from a system that regularly creates data. A series of events can also be referred to as "streaming data" or "data streams." Actions that are taken on those events include:

- Aggregations, for example, calculations such as sum, mean, standard deviation.

- Analytics, for example, forecasting a future event according to the patterns in the data.

- Transformations such as changing a number into a date format.

- Enrichment such as combining the data point with other data sources to make it more meaningful.

- Ingestion, such as inserting the data into a database

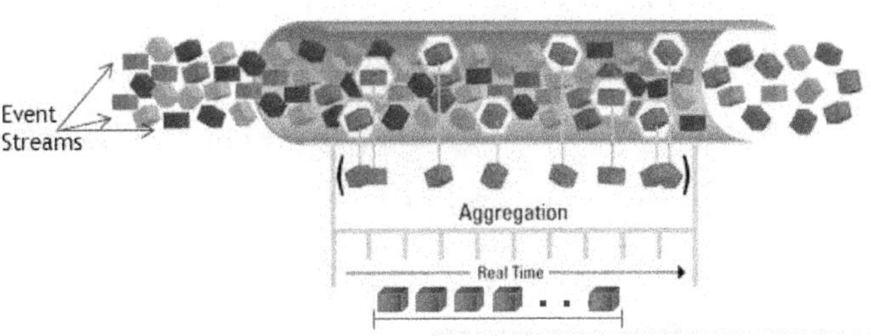


**Figure 9.1**

Complex event processing is often contemplated as related to batch processing. However, the two processes operate differently. Batch processing takes action on a broad set of static data ("data at rest"). In comparison, event processing takes action on a continuous flow of data ("data in motion"). Event stream processing is essential for situations where action needs to be taken in real-time. This is why event processing applications are often labelled as "real-time processing applications."

## How Complex Event Processing Works

CEP applications help collect a myriad of information and data while also recognizing and analyzing cause-and-effect relationships as they happen. It enables an organization to define, manage, and predict events quickly. CEP works to match incoming events against a pattern while providing insights into what is happening. It allows you to take practical actions before it's too late proactively.

In the case of CEP, an event can be anything from:

- A password change
- A stock purchase
- A transfer of funds

Complex events are generally significant business events such as opportunities or threats that surface. One of the most significant advantages of working with a CEP tool is that the events can be responded to in real-time, or as quickly as possible.

Complex event processing is mainly implemented in the following domains.

- **Business Activity Monitoring:** businesses need to identify problems and opportunities in their early stage to avoid any mishaps. Therefore, businesses use CEP to promptly determine and evaluate the essential opportunities and risks within an organization. Common examples of this process are alert notifications and fraud detection.

- **Sensory Networks:** These networks are used to track industrial facilities. Through raw numerical measurements, CEP performs this tracking function. Common examples of this method are an increase in temperature and a large amount of smoke.

- **Market Data:** These consist of stock or commodity prices, which are derived from various events. Some examples of this method are the price of gas during the first half of the year and the rise and fall of stocks once a company goes public.

Information and data within CEP are generally saved and presented within a network, database or other large systems. This information then diagnoses if there is an attack or something is underperforming, or system is having trouble operating.

CEP is used for complex continuous-intelligence applications aimed to improve situation awareness and support real-time decisions. It integrates data from various sources and uses this data to obtain events or patterns, which enables the companies to identify, control, and anticipate events, situations, and possible threats.

The events that a CEP software analyses can occur across multiple channels within a business, such as sales leads, orders, or customer service calls. The data that is fetched include text messages, weather updates, traffic reports, social media posts or stock market reports.

# STREAM PROCESSING

# Stream Processing

## What is Stream Processing?

Stream Processing is another name for Complex Event Processing. Stream processing is the practice of taking action on a stream of data, the moment the data is created. In the past, the term "real-time processing" was used by the data practitioners to refer to the data that was processed as frequently as necessary for a particular use case. However, with the introduction and implementation of stream processing technologies and frameworks, along with reduced RAM prices, "stream processing" is used in a more specific manner. Stream processing often involves numerous tasks on the incoming series of data (the "data stream"), which can be done serially, in parallel, or both. This workflow is called a stream processing pipeline that comprises of the creation of the data, the processing of the data, and the delivery of the data to a final location.

> Stream processing is the practice of taking action on a stream of data, the moment the data is created.

## How does it work?

Stream processing is most often used with the data that is created as a series of events. For example, data from IoT sensors, payment processing systems, and server and application logs. Stream processing involves publisher/subscriber (commonly referred to as pub/sub) and source/sink. Data and events are created by a publisher or source and delivered to a stream processing application, where the data is compounded, tested against fraud detection algorithms, or sometimes modified before the application sends the result to a subscriber or sink. Technically, common sources and sinks incorporate Apache Kafka®, big data repositories such as Hadoop, TCP sockets, and in-memory data grids such as Hazelcast IMDG.

## Use Cases

Use cases generally involve event data that is created due to some action, and this action needs to be responded immediately with another action. Common use cases for real-time stream processing are:

### Real-Time Fraud and Anomaly Detection

In the past, credit card providers used batch processing to perform fraud detection function. It was extremely time-consuming and was susceptible to many errors. With the advent of stream processing has many credit card providers have become able to decrease their fraud write-downs significantly. With stream processing, the entire operation has become efficient and fast. Now as soon as you swipe your card, the system runs thorough algorithms to identify and block fraudulent charges and triggers alerts for anomalous charges that require additional inspection, without holding up their customers (non-fraudulent).

> In the past, credit card providers used batch processing to perform fraud detection function.

**Internet of Things (IoT) Edge Analytics**

Different big industries such as oil and gas, transportation, and architecture, adopt stream processing to keep pace with data from billions of "things." An example of IoT data analysis is identifying peculiarities in manufacturing that specify issues to be resolved to enhance operations and increase profits. With real-time stream processing, a manufacturer may be notified that a production line is detecting too many anomalies the moment it is occurring. They can identify enormous savings and control huge waste by halting the line for immediate maintenances.

**Real-Time Personalization, Marketing and Advertising** Stream processing enables companies to provide personalised, contextual experiences for their customers. Some examples include a discount for something you added to a cart on a website but didn't immediately purchase, a suggestion to connect with a friend who just joined a social media platform or an ad for an item similar to the one you just searched for.

Stateless VS Stateful Stream Processing

In a *Stateless stream*, each event is dealt with independently from the previous events. The stream processing application treats every event the same way every time, regardless of the data, arrived beforehand.

On the contrary, *stateful stream processing* refers to a system where a state is shared between events. Hence, preceding events can impact the way current events are handled. For instance, stateful systems can monitor user sessions. This includes aggregate events coming from the same session, and output only session-level metrics when the session ends. Similarly, it can also perform aggregated counts such as counting the number of errors in every time window.

*Stateful stream processing* entails a stream processor that supports state management. Apache Flink is a framework and distributed processing engine for stateful computations over data streams. Apache Flink supports world-class stream processing, including the ability to handle enormous state size, flexible re-scaling of stateful streaming programs, state snapshots (for versioning and application updates), and upgrade and schema evolution features.

# MICROSERVICES

# Microservices

## What is Microservices?

Microservice also referred to as microservice architecture, is a unique practice of designing software applications that focuses on developing single-function modules with clearly defined operations and interfaces. Microservices has become increasingly popular since last decade because businesses now seek to become more Agile and move towards a set of practices that merge software development and IT operation. This practice is known as DevOps.

Netflix, PayPal, Amazon, Twitter eBay, Amazon, Twitter, and so forth have all progressed from monolithic to microservices architecture. Unlike microservices, a monolith application is designed as a single, autonomous unit. Hence, any modification to the application is slow because it affects the entire system. Any transformation made to a small segment of code may demand developing and implementing a completely new version of the software. Similarly, upgrading specific functions of an application may also require you to upgrade the entire application. With the introduction of microservices, these challenges of monolithic systems have been overcome because microservice architecture can become as modular as possible. In simpler terms, microservices build an application as a set of small services. Each service runs in its own process and is independently executable. Different programming languages and various data storage techniques can be used to write and store these services.

---

Netflix,
PayPal, Amazon,
Twitter eBay,
Amazon, Twitter,
and so forth have
all progressed
from monolithic
to microservices
architecture.

---

## A brief history of microservices

Martin Fowler is a British software developer, author and public speaker on software development. He has put down that "microservices" as a term was first used at a software architects' workshop in 2011 when participants found they were individually finding similar concepts in software architectures in parallel. When the group met the next year, they came up with the name microservices to describe this new concept.

James Lewis is a Principal Consultant at ThoughtWorks and member of the Technology Advisory Board. He delivered a presentation at 33rd Degree in Krakow in 2012 in a conversation entitled "Microservices—Java, the Unix Way" that defined microservices as a way to more rapidly develop software by dividing and conquering, using Conway's Law to structure teams.

This way it can be deduced that the roots of microservices connect back to three decades in the Unix world. Many people, including Martin Fowler, believe that it is more like a new spin on service-oriented architecture (SOA), a design principle that was in trend a few decades ago. Fowler recognised many of the chief features that have made microservices unique, with probably the most significant one being keeping services independent so they can be individually substituted without influencing an entire application.

He also identified such requirements as organising services around business operations and using “smart endpoints and dumb pipes,” all of which are features of “SOA done right,” as described by industry expert Greg Young during a 2016 presentation at the Microservices Conference in London.

Since that time, use of microservices has increased. Indeed, according to Fowler, microservice architectures are swiftly “becoming the default style for building enterprise applications.”

According to the conventional notion, microservices projects are suitable for executing brand-new distributed software projects. However, a recent survey by Red Hat discovered that the majority of businesses using microservices are successfully installing them to re-design legacy applications. The same study revealed that one-third of the organisations deploying microservices attain benefits within two to six months of adopting it.

## The Six Characteristics of Microservices

### 1. Multiple Components

Software that are designed as microservices can be split into various component services. So that each of these services can be installed, adjusted, and then reinstalled independently without compromising the performance of an application.

Software that are designed as microservices can be split into various component services.

Hence, you only need to modify one or more unique services rather than having to reinstall the entire applications. However, this approach does have its disadvantages, including expensive remote calls (instead of in-process calls), coarser-grained remote APIs, and even more complexity when reallocating responsibilities between components.

### 2. Built for Business

The microservices are designed, keeping in view the business capabilities and preferences. Unlike a typical monolithic development technique, where each team has a specific focus such as UIs, databases, technology layers, or server-side logic, microservice architecture works across cross-functional teams. The responsibilities of each team are to develop specific products based on one or more individual services communicating via message bus. In microservices, a team owns the product for its lifetime, as in Amazon's oft-quoted maxim "You build it, you run it."

### 3. Simple Routing

The functions of microservices are quite similar to that of the traditional UNIX system. They receive requests, process them, and generate a response accordingly. This is in contrast to the function of many other products such as ESBs (Enterprise Service Buses) work, where high-tech systems for message routing, choreography, and applying business rules are utilised. In the simplest terms, microservices have smart endpoints that process information and apply logic, and dumb pipes through which the information flows.

### 4. Decentralised

Since microservices incorporate various technologies and platforms, outdated methods of centralised control aren't ideal. Microservices community favours decentralised control mechanism because its designers strive to create useful tools that can then be used by others to solve the same problems. Similarly, microservice architecture also supports decentralised data management. Monolithic systems use a single logical database for a variety of applications. In a microservice application, each service usually manages its unique database.

### 5. Failure Resistant

Microservices are developed in such a way that they have the ability to deal with failure. Since several distinctive and varied services are interacting together, there are chances that a service could fail for multiple reasons. In such an occurrence, the client should allow its neighbouring services to perform while it withdraws from the system without disturbing the entire function. However, microservice architecture can help prevent the risk of failure. However, this requirement adds more complexity to microservices as compared to monolithic systems architecture.

Microservices are developed in such a way that they have the ability to deal with failure.

6. **Evolutionary**

Microservices architecture is an advanced design and perfect for evolutionary systems where you can't entirely predict the types of devices that your application may be accessed by. Many software programs begin with a monolithic architecture. However, as several unanticipated requirements arise, these programs can be evolved into microservices that depend on an older monolithic architecture through APIs.

## Microservices Can Increase the Efficiency of Business

If deployed effectively, microservice architectures let you upgrade your application as the number of developers working on your application increases. The key is to develop applications without creating a complicated, unwieldy beast at the macro level. It signifies that keep tracking each time a new service is added to your system or a new connection between microservices is made. It also calls for analysing the increasing complexity and making sure it is well understood. Regularly analysing the entire application system is vital to keep a unified set of microservices working effectively and reliably.

Though microservices can provide a solution for all software problems, the advantages of microservices are definitely worth it for increasing numbers of modern software organisations. By altering how software development teams are organised, companies can build teams focused on specific business services and give them both the responsibility and the authority to act as they see best. This method allows teams to rapidly move with the business as it grows according to the market demand without distorting central business activities. This arrangement alone is worth the price of deployment.

# DATABASE

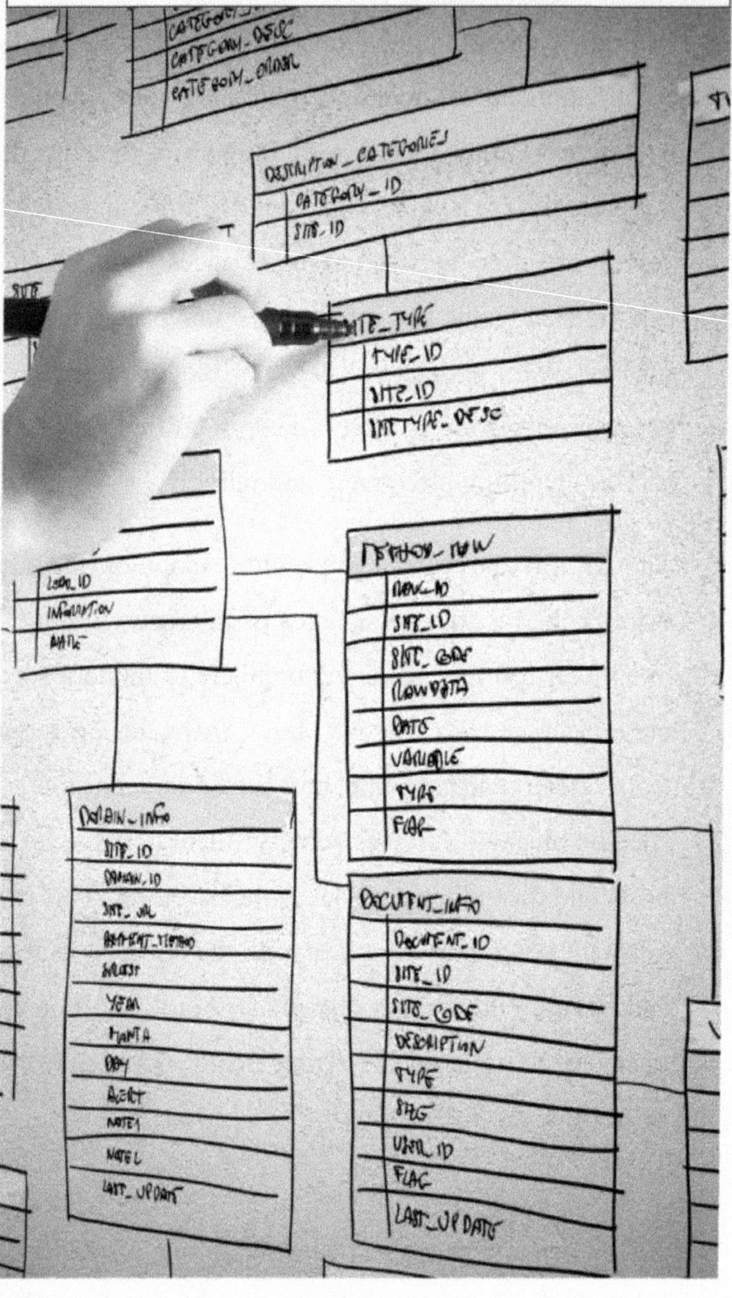

# Database

## What is Database?

The term 'database' refers to a group of records that can be administered to create useful information. The data can be retrieved, altered, managed, controlled and organised to perform various data-processing operations. The data is generally arranged across rows, columns and tables that make workload processing and data examination efficient. Different types of databases include object-oriented, relational, distributed, hierarchical, network, and others. In terms of business, databases contain mission-critical, security-sensitive, and compliance-focused record items that have complex logical relationships with other datasets and grow manifold over time as the userbase increases. Therefore, businesses require technology solutions to maintain, protect, manage and process the data stored in databases. This is where the Database Management System plays its role.

## What is Database Management System?

Database Management System (DBMS) is a technological solution used to enhance and manage the storage and access of data from databases. DBMS provides a systematic way to manage databases through an interface for users as well as workloads retrieving the databases through apps. The management responsibilities for DBMS incorporate information within the databases, the processes applied to databases (such as access and modification), and the database's logic structure. DBMS also accelerate additional organisational operations such as change management, disaster recovery, compliance, and performance monitoring.

## Benefits of Database Management System

The primary purpose for which the DBMS was designed is to solve the essential problems related to storing, managing, retrieving, securing, and auditing data in traditional file systems. Small companies prefer using spreadsheets to manage their customer data. It may be a good choice in short-term. However, as the volume of data increases, it becomes difficult to manager everything in a single spreadsheet. For example, you manage a list of customers in an excel file. A customer calls and asks you to update their data. You will open the excel file and change that particular customer's entry. However, if more than one customer call concurrently, one person will not be able to update all the data simultaneously. Databases store information more efficiently and can handle volumes of information that would be unmanageable in a spreadsheet. Spreadsheets have record limitations whereas databases do not. Compared to databases, spreadsheets may need a large amount of hard-drive space for data storage. When a spreadsheet has many fields or thousands of rows, it can be hard to read. Moreover, finding specific data can be complicated. Databases use querying tools to overcome these issues.

Following are the benefits of employing DBMS software to manage databases:

**Data security**

Through DBMS, organisations are able to implement policies that result in compliance and security. The databases are available for relevant users according to organisational policies. The DBMS system also guarantees the ideal performance of querying operations while ensuring the validity, safety and stability of data items updated to a database.

**Data sharing**

DBMS helps to create an atmosphere where end users have better access to more efficiently-managed data.

**Data access and auditing**

DBMS offers controlled access to databases according to the need of users. This controlled feature allows organisations to audit for security and compliance.

### Data integration

Instead of using a plethora of database resources, DBMS uses a single interface to manage databases with logical and physical collaborations.

### Abstraction and independence

DBMS allows organisations to transform the physical structure of database systems without having to change the logical structure that controls database relationships. Hence, organisations can upgrade storage and the infrastructure without disrupting database operations. In the same way, any modifications to the logical structure can be done without distorting the apps and services that access the databases.

### Uniform management and administration

A single control interface to perform fundamental organisational tasks makes it easy for database admins and IT users to work with data.

## Types of Database Management Systems

There are several types of database management systems. Following are the most common database management systems:

1. Hierarchical databases
2. Network databases

3. Relational databases
4. NoSQL databases

**Hierarchical Databases**

In a hierarchical database management system (hierarchical DBMSs), data is stored in a parent-children relationship node. In a hierarchical database, in addition to actual data, records also comprise information about their groups of parent/child relationships.

In a hierarchical database model, data is ordered into a tree-like structure. The data is stored in the form of a collection of fields where each field contains only one value. The records are connected through links into a parent-children relationship. In a hierarchical database system, each child record has only one parent. However, a parent can have multiple children. XML and XAML are two popular and most widely used data storages that are based on hierarchical data model.

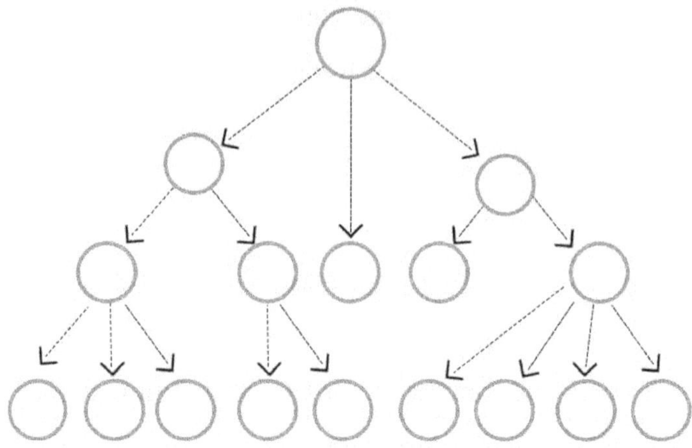

**Figure 12.1**

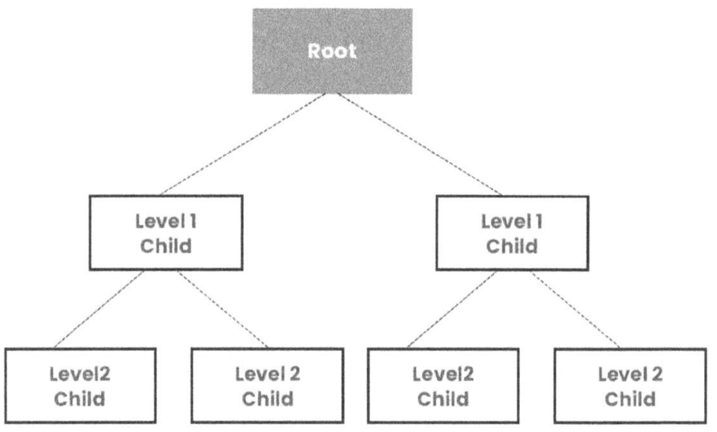


**Figure 12.2**

## Network Databases

Network database management systems (Network DBMSs) employs a network structure to build a link between entities. Network databases are primarily used on large digital computers. Network databases are also hierarchical databases. However, in a hierarchical database system, one node can have a single parent only; whereas a network node can have a link with multiple entities. A network database is similar to a cobweb or interrelated network of records.

In network databases, children are called members, and parents are called occupiers. The difference between each child or member is that it can have more than one parent. Some of the most widely used network databases are Integrated Data Store (IDS), IDMS (Integrated Database Management System), Raima Database Manager, TurboIMAGE and Univac DMS-1100.

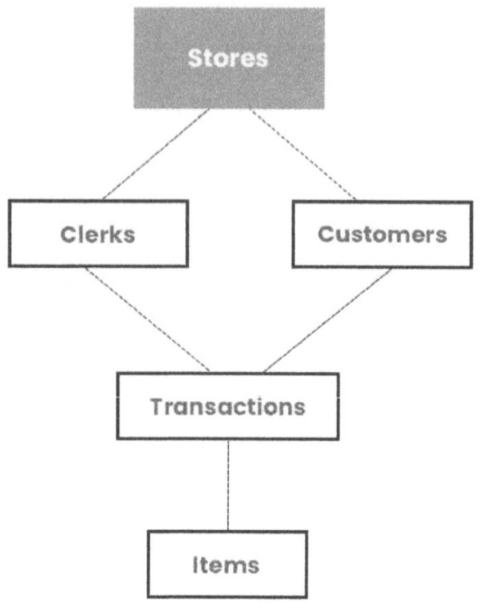


**Figure 12.3**

**Relational Databases**

In a relational database management systems (RDBMS), the link between data is relational, and data is stored in tabular form of columns and rows. Each column in a table signifies a characteristic and each row in a table represents a record. Each field in a table represents a data value.

Relational database management systems use Structured Query Language (SQL) to insert, update, delete, and search records. Relational databases work on each table that has a key field that exclusively specifies each row. These key fields can be used to link one table of data to another. Relational databases are the most widely used databases. Some of the popular RDBMS are Oracle, SQL Server, MySQL, SQLite, and IBM DB2.

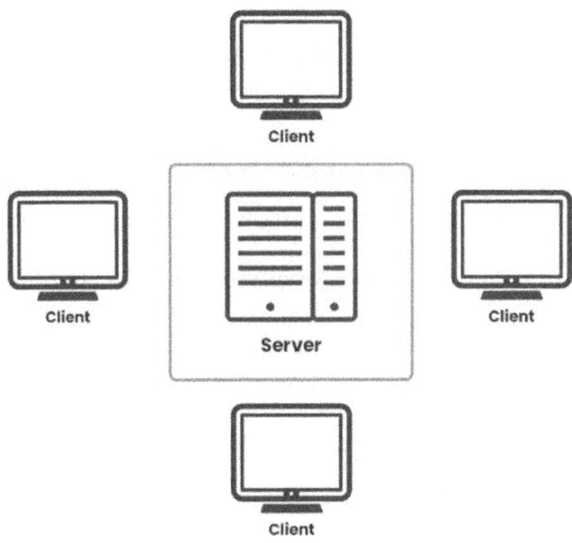


**Figure 12.4**

### NoSQL Databases

NoSQL databases are the databases that do not use SQL as their primary data access language. Graph database, network database, object database, and document databases are common NoSQL databases. NoSQL database does not have preset structures. This is the reason NoSQL databases are ideal for rapidly changing development environments.

NoSQL lets developers make modifications without affecting applications. NoSQL databases can be characterised in five major categories, namely, Column, Document, Graph, Key-value, and Object databases.

The top ten popular databases are:

1. Cosmos DB (Multi-model database)
2. ArangoDB (Multi-model database)
3. Couchbase Server (Multi-model database)
4. CouchDB (Document oriented database)
5. Amazon DocumentDB (Document oriented database)
6. MongoDB (Document oriented database)
7. Elasticsearch (Document oriented database)
8. Informix (Object oriented database)
9. SAP HANA (Column oriented database)
10. Neo4j (Graph database)

# Criticism

The concept of design patterns has been severely criticised by some individuals in the field of computer science.

## Targets the Wrong Problem

According to Paul Graham's essay Revenge of the Nerds, the need for design patterns results from using computer language or techniques with inadequate abstraction ability. Under ideal factoring, any concept must not be copied but simply referenced. However, if something is referenced rather than copied, then there is no 'design pattern' to label and catalogue. Peter Norvig too provides a similar argument. Peter demonstrates that 16 out of the 23 patterns in the Design Patterns book (which is primarily focused on C++) are simplified or eliminated (via direct language support) in Lisp or Dylan.

## Lacks Formal Foundations

The study of design patterns has been markedly ad hoc. Some have argued that the concept dramatically needs to be put on a more formal footing. At OOPSLA 1999, the Gang of Four were (with their full cooperation) were subjected to a show trial in which they were "charged" with several crimes against computer science. They were "convicted" by ⅔ of the "jurors" who attended the trial.

## Leads to Inefficient Solutions

The idea behind design patterns is an attempt to standardise what is already accepted as the best practice. Mainly this may appear to be extremely beneficial. However, in practice, it results in the redundant duplication of code. It is always a more effective solution to use a well-factored implementation instead of "just barely good enough" design pattern.

www.ingramcontent.com/pod-product-compliance
Ingram Content Group UK Ltd.
Pitfield, Milton Keynes, MK11 3LW, UK
UKHW020424250726
13967UKWH00007B/2797

9 781914 264115